Sagebrush Gunnysacks and Bailing Wire

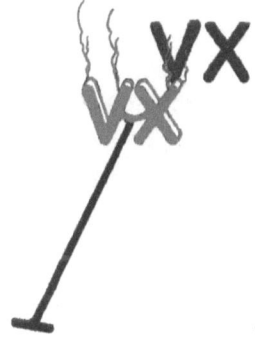

Grace Vyvey Gregory

Grandma's Cabin Books
Encampment, Wyoming

Published by

Grandma's Cabin Books
Encampment, Wyoming 82325

ISBN 978-1-941694-00-8
©2015 Grandma's Cabin Books

CONTENTS

Prologue	....	v
Dedication	....	vi
Acknowledgments	....	vii
Introduction	....	ix
Chapter I:	Bobbin Lace to Sagebrush..........	1
Chapter II:	The Homestead........................	9
Chapter III:	New Arrivals in the Valley..........	13
Chapter IV:	Emma Alone............................	19
Chapter V:	The Neighbors........................	21
Chapter VI:	Catastrophes..........................	27
Chapter VII:	Smokehouse and Cellar.............	33
Chapter VIII:	The Potato Patch and Mother's Garden......	37
Chapter IX:	Badges of Courage....................	41
Chapter X:	Broken Bones and Bloody Noses........	47
Chapter XI:	Troubled 20's and Early 30's.........	61
Chapter XII:	Harnessing the Wind..................	67
Chapter XIII:	The Blizzard of '49....................	71
Chapter XIV:	Trips to the Old Country.............	75
Chapter XV:	The Last Years........................	89
Epilogue	....	94
About the Author	....	97

Prologue

"Nothing now is left but majestic memory." – Longfellow

Death caught the Author with her book in rough draft form. According to her last wishes, her book has been completed and published. The actual text of this book is reproduced as it was written by Grace Vyvey Gregory.

Her daughter, Sharyn Gregory Guthridge, wishes to express to all who read the pages herein that one can only ponder at what has been "lost forever during one turn of this world of ours."

Dedication

This book is dedicated to the author, Grace Carol Vyvey Gregory, and her two grandchildren, Gregory and Tifney, without whom this book would never have been written.

ACKNOWLEDGMENTS

TO THOSE WHO LIVED THESE EVENTS

The Verplanckes
Peter and Emma
Alice
Butch
Lena
Lillian
Sam

The Vyveys
Charles and Emma
Bert
Carl
Fox
Grace
John
René

TO THOSE WHO PROVIDED INFORMATION AND PICTURES

The Verplancke-Vyvey Children
Phyllis Everist Vyvey
Cheryl Vyvey Wieburg
Erma Platt Logan
John Billiaert

To the co-editor who provided her expertise and moral support
Jane Logan Dorn

To the Illustrator
Jim Beasley

For Cover Design
Ray Guthridge, Jr.

Edited and Compiled by
Sharyn Gregory Guthridge

INTRODUCTION

Countless times through the years, I have had the desire to record the life and times of my parents. Until now, I never did anything about it, mainly, I suppose, because the question would always come to mind, "Who would be interested?" The last few years this desire has become stronger, especially when our family donated to the Encampment Museum in Encampment, Wyoming, their picture as a memorium. Ever since that time, I have wondered how many times the curator at the museum has been asked, "But who were they?"

Recently, my two grandchildren asked me, "Who were your mother and father, Granny?" This is my effort to answer their question. In so doing, I am tapping the button that activates my memory bank and will let the pen in my hand record what my brain has stored these many years. Also, I will touch the memories of my five brothers and two half-brothers before it is too late and the memories are lost forever during one turn of this world of ours.

Grace C. Vyvey Gregory
Rawlins, Wyoming 1981

I
Bobbin Lace to Sagebrush

My mother, Emma Marie Vermeersch, was born October 17, 1884, in Westkapelle, Belgium, a small village in North Flanders near the Holland border. I know very little about her childhood except she had brothers and sisters and was very poor as so many were around the turn of the century in Europe.

Many times she would tell me of growing up and skating on the canal that separated Belgium from Holland. Every Thursday her family took their farm produce, laces and what-have-you to Westkapelle Day in the marketplace in the nearby big city of Bruges. It is one of the oldest cities in Europe. Its art treasure, architecture, walls around the city, canals, many bridges, some only large enough for a donkey to cross (for which its name stands) are very well known around the world. The small villages within walking distance each had their day of the week to sell their wares in the marketplace in the center of the city. This practice still continues in Belgium.

Emma lived with her grandmother most of the time, and at a very early age she was taught by her grandmother and her mother the art of knitting and making the famous Belgium bobbin lace. These articles were her contributions on the family's day at the weekly market. She was raised a Catholic and looked forward to the market day because she could attend church in Bruges Cathedral in the early morning before the day of selling began.

One of her fondest memories, one that she held dear to her heart, was being privileged to take part in the Procession of the Blood on the Feast day of the Sacred Heart in June in Bruges when she was fifteen years old. On that day, she was one of those to kiss the Vial of Blood which was brought to Bruges by Count Diedrich of Alsace, after one of his four crusades to the Holy Land. This relic of the Precious Blood is venerated to this day. It is still kept in the basilica of the Precious Blood and housed in a shrine more than four feet high. It is believed to be blood shed on the cross by Christ and it is also believed by some to liquefy on Good Friday and again congeal on Easter Sunday every year.

When I visited Belgium many years ago, I went on a tour from Ostende to hear the beautiful Concert of the Bells of the churches in Bruges. The tour narrator was a young, English-speaking woman who told us that during World War II when it was imminent that Belgium would again be overrun by the Germans, the United States offered to fly the precious vial to the United States for safekeeping until the war was over. The offer was refused by Belgium and the vial was hidden for four years in one of the canals running through the city. It was never found by the Germans. After the war, it was retrieved by the Belgians and again placed in the Basilica of the Precious Blood where it remains today.

At the age of seventeen, my mother left her grandmother's home and went to a nearby city, Moerkerke, some five mile distant, and obtained work as a maid for a wealthy family. Emma had long, dark brown hair, blue eyes and stood five feet three inches tall and weighed less than a hundred weight.

Everyday, she would have a few hours to herself, and she would spend this time making bobbin lace, knitting or making wares to take to the marketplace for extra money.

One particular day, she sat alone on a straight-backed chair in the yard of her employer's home under a pear tree making the lace. In her deep concentration as her fingers flew with the bobbins and thread making the bobbin lace strip that was running down off her lap, she didn't see the young man watching her. He took the bobbins and lace from her hands and tossed it aside saying, "You will never again have to make lace." She was furiously startled seeing her work only a tangle of thread and bobbins on the ground. Before her stood a huge man, six and a half feet tall, slim, straight and nineteen years her senior. She had heard of this young man who was home from America visiting his parents, but she had never met him. This encounter changed the course of her entire life.

During their brief courtship, he told her what her new home, her new life, would be like. He told her of America and the land there he had homesteaded and it would be all theirs to make a home and raise a family. They first met in the fall of 1901 and on February 22, 1902, they were married in Emma's parish church in Moerkerke, Belgium.

Emma Marie Vermeersch was now Mrs. Peter John Verplancke. They went from Moerkerke to Peter's home, a small farm near St. Kruis, Belgium. They lived there from the time of the marriage until the end of the year 1902, while Peter was disposing of his interests

Wedding Picture - Emma and Peter Verplancke

in Belgium. Then they boarded ship at Zeebruge, Belgium, a port on the North Sea, to sail to the United States.

They were aboard ship three and a half weeks. Emma was violently seasick most of the way. In a storm, when a huge beam in the ship gave way and missed her only by inches as it fell, she knew she would never be a good sailor. The days dragged for her during the crossing. She would never forget her elation when they docked in New York City.

From New York City Peter and Emma entrained for a few day sojourn in Chicago. They traveled on to St. Louis to visit a short while with Peter's brother, Leo. In early March, they left St. Louis by rail for Wyoming and the homestead. They arrived in Walcott, Wyoming, a few days later. When they boarded the stagecoach for their last forty miles to Riverside, there was just one seat left. Emma rode inside the coach and Peter rode outside on top of the coach with the luggage.

Also making the trip from St. Louis was a young man from St. Andres, Belgium, who was going to find work in the Riverside-Encampment area. His name was Leo Hillewaert. Leo was twenty-four years old but was no bigger in stature than a twelve-year-old boy. He was to go with them to the homestead and stay with them until he got work in the smelter that was operating in Encampment. This young man was to share in an important event in Emma's life many years later. He worked in the smelter until it closed down and then moved to Craig, Colorado, where he, too, homesteaded, married and raised a family.

Stagecoach to Encampment in early days.

Panorama view of Encampment

On March 16, 1903, Emma and Peter Verplancke and Leo Hillewaert arrived in mid-afternoon in Riverside, ten miles from the homestead she was so anxious to reach. Peter had written a letter from St. Louis to the hired man, Richard Pelz, in charge of the homestead. He was to meet them to take them on home. The hired man was not there when they arrived. The proprietor of the small grocery store, Sam Morgan, and A. J. Anderson, a clerk at the store and a friend of Peter's, were the first two people my mother met upon her arrival in the Encampment valley.

Emma was determined to get to their destination. She insisted that they would start out walking and would meet the hired man on his way to fetch them home. Against the advice and concern of all present because of a storm threading its way down from the mountain, her excitement and curiosity to see her new home won the argument of walking the last ten miles of their long journey home.

This trio, Peter, the big, stalwart man, Emma, a tiny slip of a woman in a long, bustled dress, high button shoes, heavy coat and fancy hat, and Leo, very little larger than she, with the accordion he would not leave behind, slung over his shoulder, walked down the road to meet the hired man. After walking a few miles, they decided the hired man must not have received the letter, or didn't know what day it was. They watched the storm coming ever closer. When they were halfway to the Brownlee's place, which was about six miles from Riverside, they were walking in a foot of new snow. Shortly past this point, the early spring blizzard engulfed them. The howling wind and swirling snow reduced visibility to zero.

The cold bit into their faces, feet and hands, as the snow began to pile into drifts. It was very difficult to walk. They trudged on until Peter could see Emma and Leo were tiring. They were making much slower headway. Peter knew they would have to make it to the Brownlee's place and spend the night there. They hid the accordion behind a large sagebrush to be retrieved later.

Peter realized they had to keep moving so they stumbled on. They reached the point where Emma and Leo were exhausted. Peter picked them both up, one under each arm, and pushed on up the slopes. He would set them down and make them walk down the rolling hillsides. They pressed on in this fashion. Finally, at midnight, the buildings of the Brownlee's place were before them and the last few hundred yards were sheltered some by the trees along the frozen creek bed. Peter carried them into the kitchen where coffee was brewing on the wood cook stove. It was an aroma Emma never forgot. It was here she learned what to do for frostbite and half-frozen limbs. Her face, ears and hands were frostbitten and her feet and legs were half frozen. Quickly and efficiently, Mrs. Brownlee piled snow over the half-frozen areas. Hot soup and tea was all Emma could have these first few hours and then the discomfort and fear lessened. It was very difficult for her to believe that they were still four or five miles from their home. Breakfast was huge, but the ordeal was not yet at its conclusion.

The next morning Mr. Brownlee sent his son-in-law, Doc Culleton, to the Peter Verplancke place to tell the hired man where the Verplanckes were and to hitch up a sled and team and come for them. There was no one home at the homestead so Doc left a note on the kitchen table. The storm was still raging in all its fierce velocity and after waiting all that day and the next, there was no sight of the hired man with the sled. The morning of the third day, a slight break in the weather was thought to be observed and Peter borrowed a sled and team of horses from Mr. Brownlee to continue their journey home. Peter was determined to fire the hired man on sight. Doc Culleton accompanied them so he could return the sled and team.

Emma and Leo were comfortably placed in the sled, and surrounded with heated rocks and flatirons tucked in the blankets around them. The blizzard was not over. Halfway between the two places, visibility once again reached zero in the swirling and wind-driven snow. Disaster was averted in the nick of time by the dexterity and horsemanship of Peter. In one split second, a team and sled coming head on at a high rate of speed appeared before them. Peter averted a head-on collision in the blizzard between his team of horses and the hired man's team of horses who was finally coming to get them at the Brownlee place. After quieting the horses and organizing things once again, they put the hired man and his team in front and Peter followed closely behind. They reasoned that the team in front knew their way home.

So it was that Emma, Peter and Leo reached the homestead three and a half days after leaving Riverside, a distance of only nine miles. Emma was to remark the next day, "Yesterday was hell, today it is heaven." The date they arrived at the homestead was March 20, 1903.

II   The Homestead

    Years later, mother was to tell me of her first impression and discoveries about her new world. The first surprise was her home, built all of logs with a dirt roof and board floors. Houses were never built of wood in her homeland. The part of Belgium she came from was far below sea level and dampness was always present. Wood rotted quickly. Buildings there were built of stone, brick and mortar, and stood for centuries in that climate. Every building here was log: house, barn, chicken house, sheds, corrals and the buck'n rail fences.

Original Verplancke homestead.

As she stepped out of her front door that first morning, she found the storm of the past few days was spent. She found a white world for miles around and the brightest blue sky she had ever seen. The sun was warm and the snow melted quickly and soon that day everything turned to mud puddles and slush. The day before she couldn't see beyond arm's length, but this day she could see miles and miles of rolling hills and draws covered everywhere with sagebrush. The only water nearby was from the pump attached to the very strange looking and noisy windmill, perched high on one end of the house. There was not a tree close by, but the Sierra Madre Mountain Range to the south was beautiful in its blanket of snow.

It was spring! It was time to plow and plant seeds for that year's crop. Grain, hay and potatoes and, of course, the ever-present garden. Peter hitched up the horse to the walking plow one morning and began plowing the garden spot for her. The horse was balky and obstinate and she could hear Peter shouting and instructing him in his duties, calling his name quite often. She ran from the house to tell Peter that she thought the horse had the most beautiful name she had ever heard. She repeated it over and over – "Son-of-a-Bitch, Son-of-a-Bitch, Son-of-a-Bitch." These were the first words she learned in English. When Peter laughed uproariously, she knew she had made a big mistake.

After the garden spot was readied, Peter and Emma planted rows of seeds together in the evenings. A generous neighbor gave them shoots of raspberries, currants, and gooseberries. After the planting, the garden was in Emma's care.

Peter's daylight-to-dark days were spent in the small fields of hay and grain and clearing more ground of the sagebrush that grew everywhere. This was no easy task. He burned the sagebrush, plowed it up and burned it again and again. There was no native grass on his homestead. Every acre had to be cleared of the sagebrush, and the roots went deep into the ground. Before alfalfa or grains could be planted, Peter had to plow and burn, rake and burn, level and burn.

After the planting, when the shoots of hay and grain came up, the battle for water began. Peter knew water for the stock and for his crops were his major problem on this land. The sagebrush land was rich; good soil and alfalfa fields made it even richer and grain in abundance could be raised on it, but without water, everything would dry up and burn during the growing season and there would be no harvest for the long winter months. He knew the answer to the problem was obvious. The homestead lay a short distance from the foothills of the nearby mountain range. Heavy snows in the mountains fed the spring run–

off just before the growing season began. Peter would build a large reservoir across the small Antelope Creek that ran down through the homestead, and store the spring run-off. He would then use it wisely and well during the growing season to irrigate the crops. This was very odd to both Emma and Peter who came from a country where water was held back by dykes and canals of water ran everywhere, along with mist and gray rainy skies most of the time. Here in the new country, water rights and a reservoir had top priority in every sense of the word. They directed all their efforts to the construction of a reservoir those first few years on the homestead.

The neighbors were very helpful in trading work and machinery. The womenfolk helped each other with the coming of new babies, since a doctor was very seldom in attendance on these occasions. The menfolk would help each other build the fences and ditches and exchange help harvesting the grain crops each fall.

But, in the spring, when irrigating the crops would begin, there were always some disgruntled spats among them. Each man was always sure his neighbor was helping himself to the water, and when the fences were built, each was equally sure the fence was not on the boundary line and his neighbor had snitched a few feet here and there.

Such was the case when a neighbor rode in on horseback one morning to the Verplancke yard and a terrible argument immediately ensued between him and Peter. In the house, Emma could hear their voices rising louder and louder. As the argument became more heated and angry words flew back and forth, she stepped to the kitchen door to see what it was all about. As she stood there, she saw the hired men nearby, open-mouthed as the argument grew more heated between Peter and the man on horseback. She saw the man on horseback take down his lariat from the saddle on his horse and in a flash, throw a wide loop and rope Peter, pinning Peter's arms tight to his sides. As he whirled the horse around, Peter was jerked off his feet and dragged across the yard.

Emma sprinted from the door, grabbed the axe from the chopping block by the woodpile and as the rope dragging Peter was stretched tight over a log in the yard, with one stroke of the axe, she cut the rope in two, freeing Peter. With the axe still in her hands, she flew toward the man on horseback who rode for home as fast as his horse could go. Her quick thinking and spontaneous reaction had averted a terrible catastrophe for both men.

Emma's feat was never forgotten by those witnessing the event and it was told over and over down through the years. Emma never made any comment but whenever it was mentioned within her hearing, a flash of terror would cross her face as the memory of the event swept over her. The subject was quickly changed and forgotten.

The animosity was forgotten and again, Peter and the neighbor worked together after the episode. Sometime later this neighbor sold his sagebrush homestead to a newcomer and moved from the valley.

Peter and Emma's first child, a daughter, Helena Germania, was born that fall, late in November of 1903. She was born in the log house with a neighbor's wife acting as midwife.

Emma was more or less confined to the house that first winter which was fairly mild as far as winters in Wyoming are concerned. Her only outings were to nearby Downington for the mail once a week or when Peter would take her there in a sled or buggy, whichever was appropriate, and the weather would permit. There was a post office and small grocery store there as nearby Beaver Creek was also getting pretty well settled and a small mine or two was in operation close by. George Condict was the mail driver at that time carrying the mail from Encampment to Downington and on to Pearl, Colorado. Emma and Peter also made trips to Encampment and Riverside for staples and supplies. These two small towns were bustling with mining activities and the inhabitants were of all nationalities and walks of life, lured there by the gold and copper mines.

A copper smelter was operating in Encampment and the world's longest aerial tramway was built for the mines to Encampment to bring the ore to the smelter where it was melted down into ingots to be shipped out on the Union Pacific Railroad spur that had been built from Walcott to the Saratoga and Encampment valleys. Peter still had his hired man, Richard Pelz, with them. He, too, was a Belgian and therefore, Flemish was spoken most of the time on the homestead. Emma's English was very slow in coming those first few years and she was quite unable to visit with anyone she met. With her dictionary of the two languages, she was to learn to read the new language before she spoke English and dropped the Belgian tongue forever. (Emma also spoke Walloon.)

Peter and Emma were kept busy with the work of wrestling a living from their land and building a reservoir so sorely needed to make progress as well as building the fences and buildings around the place.

The family was growing too, with another daughter, Alice Elizabeth, arriving in October, 1905, and their first son, Lucien Peter, nicknamed Sam, was born in December, 1906. Lillian Mary, their third daughter, was born in 1908.

III
New Arrivals in the Valley

Early in 1907, a young couple and their family arrived in the Encampment valley from Michigan. They were Julia and Ed Taeckens and they had originally come from Eernegem, Belgium, a small farming village on the outskirts of Ostende, a Belgian seaport resort on the North Sea and English Channel. A few weeks later, Julia's brother, Charles Louis Vyvey, arrived at his sister's home in Riverside. Charles and Ed got jobs working in the smelter in Encampment in March of 1907.

Charles was born January 8, 1884, in Eernegem, Belgium. At 23, he had followed his youngest sister to America by stowing away on a freighter. After about three or four days at sea, Charles was discovered. To pay for his passage, he was put to work as caretaker of the Belgian draft horses being brought into the United States. He had been aboard the freighter six weeks and came down the St. Lawrence River and docked in Detroit, Michigan. Then, he came by train from Detroit to Walcott and on to Riverside by stagecoach.

Charles was a sturdily built man, five feet six inches tall with coal black hair, blue eyes, and always wore a smile on his face.

Charles fired the furnaces in the smelter and despite a crippled arm, he was able to perform these duties very well. He obtained lodging and batched in a small log cabin in Riverside with several Swedes who also were working at the smelter. All went well with this arrangement until Charles went to the nearby grocery store to obtain staples a few weeks later. One can only imagine his chagrin, frustration and mirth when he discovered he was not learning to speak English, but instead, Swedish.

By this time, there were a number of Belgians in the bustling Encampment-Riverside vicinities. Activities were numerous and everyone got to know everyone else. Some of the Belgians were the Peter Verplanckes, homesteading on Antelope Creek, Ed and Julia Taeckens, Al LaRoy, Richard Pelz, Louis Kuntz, Charles Vyvey, Leo Hillewaert and the Leo Verplanckes who had moved out from St. Louis, Missouri. It was inevitable that they would all meet and know

Charles Louis Vyvey

each other all their lives even though some of them were to leave the valley and make their fortunes elsewhere in America.

Eventually, Julia Taeckens' husband, Ed, returned to Belgium and never returned to America. Nothing whatsoever was ever learned about what happened to him. Julia later obtained a divorce and married Willard Hayden and they took up a homestead adjoining the Peter Verplanckes as did Louis Kuntz and Al LaRoy. The Leo

Verplanckes and young Leo Hillewaert left the area and went to Craig Colorado, and took up homesteads there side by side.

After many years, Leo Verplancke sold his holdings in Colorado to Leo Hillewaert and he and his family moved back to St. Louis, Missouri, where he lived out the remainder of his life.

They all had their problems with the English language because of their close association with each other since they spoke only their native tongue among themselves. But they also had their language problems even among themselves. They had come here from different areas of Belgium and Belgium is a bilingual nation. Walloon is spoken in one section and Flemish in another. Charles and his sister, Julia, spoke Flemish and some French and Peter and Emma and Leo Hillewaert spoke Walloon and all of them were striving to learn English. They all eventually did learn English, but only one, Emma Verplancke, never again spoke her native tongue once she had mastered the English language. In fact, she forgot it completely and could not remember it even if she tried. She had put it completely out of her life.

Emma had learned to drive a team of horses and when the need arose, she would help in the fields during the haying season and rake hay for a few hours. She also had started taking the horse and buggy, making the trip to nearby Downington or to Riverside and Encampment, for the mail and groceries and supplies as needs dictated. She would take the children with her on these outings in the buggy with the top up to shade the children and the baby in a bushel basket riding at her feet. The buggy was beautiful – black with black fringe, a red pin stripe and sported red spoked wheels.

It was from one of these outings to town that Emma returned to her home to find a frightened little black girl in the yard. You can just imagine her chagrin when she realized this little black child was her own daughter. Her eldest son, Sam, had seen fit to crop Lillian's hair, and using soot from the woodstove, had covered her from head to toe. To complete the transition, her hair had been tightly curled with the curling iron.

Peter and his helpers worked every spare moment building the reservoir to store the spring run-off of water from the mountains. Finally, it was finished. One of the neighbor's children crawled through the pipe from one end to the other when it was finished, but he said it was a close squeak in one place. Then it was put into use. Shortly thereafter, Peter discovered that the dam had caved in the pipe and the reservoir was useless. The slips, fresnos and shovels were again put to use immediately to remove the mountains of earth fill from the collapsed pipe and a new pipe was installed. Once again, in 1909, the reservoir was completed and put into use.

However, before the reservoir could be effectively used to store the spring run-off, a ditch from the mountains above to the flatlands below had to be built. Peter and six of the neighbors decided to take their picks and shovels and go into the mountains to dig this ditch. They agreed that the water thus channeled to their land below would be divided into seven equal shares. They took with them a surveyor to help in locating the best possible placement of the ditch.

After the surveyor finished his work the seven men began to dig. After a great deal of labor and sweat the ditch was completed, but the men soon discovered that the surveyor had been wrong – the last couple of hundred yards of the ditch, the water would have to run uphill! The Goliath Peter grabbed up his pick and shovel and *singlehandedly* dug out the new two hundred yards of ditch. Because of his lone feat of labor and the respect it commanded, the Verplancke homestead was to hold from that day forward, not just one share of the water, but two and a half shares. The Billy Creek Ditch, as it was named, is to this day a major transport of water to the irrigation of the farmland below.

Thus, this ditch and the reservoir are still in use today, still serving their much needed purpose, seventy years later. The fields were growing too, as the sagebrush was cleared. Oats, barley, and alfalfa patches were turning the sagebrush land into green fields and a potato patch of several acres was also producing very well.

In the fall, after the hay and grain harvest, the potatoes were dug from their long neat rows, sacked in one hundred pound gunnysacks and delivered to the Mossman Grocery Store in Walden, Colorado, a distance of some fifty miles by freight wagon and a six-horse team. On the return trip the winter supply of groceries and staples was aboard the freight wagon. Flour, sugar, rice, beans, crackers, canned vegetables and fruits, dried fruits of all kinds, fresh apples, and oranges in their bushel baskets were the barter for the potatoes every year.

Each year, Emma's garden grew larger and the currants, raspberries, gooseberries, and a new strawberry patch produced more and more. A cellar and an icehouse were added to the row of buildings, and in the winter, ice was harvested from the reservoir in blocks and stored in sawdust in the icehouse for summer use.

In 1908, the smelter in Encampment closed down forever, partly due to poor management and lack of foresight of the owners. More and more of the area's inhabitants chose to work on the farms and cattle ranches springing up along the Encampment and Platte rivers running through the area. Charles Vyvey, along with many others, was out of work, and so he found work in the Hog Park and French Creek tie camps. In the spring of 1909, he made the tie drive with his Swedish friends down the Platte River to Fort Fred Steele, some fifty miles down river. The tie drive was a yearly event. The ties were used on the Union Pacific Railroad.

After the 1909 tie drive when Charles was again out of work, he went to the Hayden and Verplancke homesteads and went to work for Peter Verplancke. Charles, too, had been raised on a small farm in Belgium so that this work was neither strange nor unwelcome. He had worked with horses all his young life before coming to America. As time went on, it became obvious that Charles was very adept at handling the spirited and unpredictable Tortan horses and he assumed more and more of the freighting duties with the six-horse teams. He freighted the grain and potatoes south to Walden, Colorado, or to Saratoga, Wyoming.

So it was that on the morning of October 31, 1909, the hired men were busy loading the freight wagon with oats for railroad crews building the railroad to Walden. Charles was harnessing and hitching up the six-horse team to the freight wagon for the five-day round trip. Peter hitched up a spirited team of horses to a light spring wagon and went hurriedly to get Julia Hayden to assist Emma with the coming of a new baby and to help with the older children. Shortly thereafter, the men heard the pounding of runaway horses and the screams of a woman and children. Julia and two of her children were in the wagon the runaway horses were pulling in their flight across the fields. The men caught the horses and Julia told them what had happened. Peter had loaded them in the wagon and they had started back when they stopped to close the gate to the Hayden place. The noise of the gate dragging on the frozen ground spooked the team and they bolted. Peter tried to get the driving reins of the team by jumping into the wagon, but as he grabbed the front of the wagon to leap inside, the board broke under the big man's weight and he fell in the path of the wagon wheels as the horses ran in their fright. He was run over by the wagon where he fell and that was where Charles found him writhing in agony from his injuries.

Charles knew he could not load the big man into the wagon by himself, so he went back to the Verplancke place and sent a man to fetch Doctor Monahan as quickly as possible. He then hitched a horse to the stoneboat and went for Peter. He placed Peter on the stoneboat and pulled him to the Verplancke's front door. Charles, by himself, carried Peter through the door and laid him on the bed. Emma had only a few moments to see Peter before giving birth to their second son, William Joseph Verplancke.

Charles knew how vital it was that the oats, already loaded on the freight wagon, be delivered to Walden before it got any colder or a freezing snow came. All would be lost. So, he climbed aboard the freight wagon and started out on his journey. All he could do here was done.

Dr. Monahan arrived and a careful examination of Peter revealed a broken pelvis and extensive internal injuries. It was imperative they get him to a hospital as quickly as possible. Arrangements were made to put Peter aboard the train at Encampment for the trip to the hospital in Cheyenne early the next morning.

Later in the evening of that first day, a priest for the Catholic Church in Rawlins, 70 miles away, arrived at the homestead, the first priest Emma was to meet in this country. This priest administered the Sacrament of the Sick to Peter, after which he baptized the new baby, William Joseph and the four other children conditionally, as Emma had done this for them herself at times of illness during their young years.

Peter was put on the train the next morning for Cheyenne. He died in the hospital in Cheyenne on November 7, 1909. His body was returned to Encampment and buried in the Encampment cemetery. The date was November 9, 1909.

Charles, the hired man, returned home from his long freighting journey to Walden, the day after Peter died. The freight was loaded with the staples Peter had ordered for the long winter ahead. It was on that day Charles learned of Peter's death and impending funeral.

IV

Emma Alone

So it was that Emma Verplancke became a widow at the age of twenty-five with five children to raise. The oldest child, Helena, was nearing her sixth birthday and the youngest, William, was only a few days old.

Emma was still very isolated on the homestead and could not speak English well enough to take care of the burdens falling upon her shoulders. The tender years of her children demanded most of her time and attention. All of them were striving to learn English and Helena was to start school the next fall. Speaking half Belgian and half English, school was a trial for Helena and the others that were to follow. With the help of the Belgian hired hands the work of raising the crops and clearing the land of sagebrush continued on the homestead.

Emma started proceedings to settle Peter's estate and truly found out how devastating her position was without the English language at her command and her lack of knowledge concerning the settlement of an estate.

There was very little money and creditors were everywhere. There wasn't any way she could meet their demands. She wanted only to go home to Belgium with her children. She wrote her relatives there and asked if they could help her with the arrangement. When she received their reply, she was told that they could not help her, and if she did not have a lot of money, it was best that she stay where she was. Emma stayed and continued her struggle for survival for her children and herself.

V
The Neighbors

Slowly, Emma began to get acquainted with her neighbors on Beaver Creek: the Wilbur Toothakers, the Frank Burgesses, the Brownlee's, the Rahlmans, Will Hunter, Henry Flohr, J.R. Bingham, Ike Platt and his family, the Haydens and the Chan Forney's. She became acquainted with a young married couple, Ralph and Awilda Platt early in 1909. They had moved back to the Platt ranch in 1908 to take over management for Ralph's father, Ike. Emma and Awilda were to form a life-long friendship and this friendship still exists in the third generations. Later, one of Awilda's sons, Wayne Platt, married one of Emma's, granddaughters, Georgia Romios (Alice Verplancke's daughter) and henceforth Awilda's grandchildren were also Emma's great grandchildren. These children still live on the Platt Ranch today, seventy years later, not over a mile east of Emma's home. More recently, Pete Romios' son, Bill married Awilda's great niece Aurilla Condict, and this young family lives on the Romios ranch, not over a mile west of Emma's home. (See map)

Emma's command of the native tongue was to become better and better through this association and the children's entrance into the world of learning at the nearby Beaver Creek school. Peter had helped to cut and haul the logs for the building of this school in the late 1890's prior to returning to Belgium and marrying Emma. As she once remarked, "My children helped me learn to speak the English language. I actually learned it from my children."

School functions and neighbors' get-togethers were to mean a great deal to Emma and were looked forward to with great anticipation each year.

Beaver Creek School painting by author.

Through association with these neighbors, the hired help of Emma's also were learning the language and it was being spoken more and more at the homestead.

However, the legal aspects of Peter's estate were getting more and more into a tangled state of affairs through Emma's absorption in caring for the five children and her isolation from Rawlins, her attorney, and the courthouse there. It became a day-to-day existence and tomorrow was only a thought even more illusive than a ray of light from a rainbow in the sky. Occasionally, she would receive a most welcome letter from her relatives in Belgium, which she read and reread over and over. Two of the Belgium men helping the Verplancke and Hayden families, Al LaRoy and Charles Vyvey, both took up homesteads nearby. Al's homestead was on DuFunny Creek, a few miles distant to the west, and Charles' adjoined the Verplancke's on the south.

As time went by, a new life, a new marriage was opening up for Emma and Charles together. In May of 1911, they were married and Emma was now Mrs. Charles L. Vyvey.

Charles and Emma Vyvey wedding picture.

    Emma and Charles had so much in common. There was only nine months difference in their ages, and they came from the same country, same environment and both had the same sense of humor and wit. Strange that these two people would meet so far from their homeland of Belgium, marry and go forward together.

    Charles had come from a large family having two living sisters, three half-brothers and two half-sisters in Belgium. His family were farmers in Eernegem, Belgium. Charles' mother had died when he was an infant, and a nurse in charge of the family had somehow dropped him and twisted his arm in the shoulder socket. His hand faced outward instead of inward. When he had first stepped off the freighter from Belgium, he had been asked by a Customs Officer to pass a physical examination. This consisted of shaking hands with the Customs Officer using both hands. Charles shook the officer's hand using his right hand and when it came time to shake using his left hand, a friend of Charles' put his hand under Charles' arm and shook the officer's hand. Thus, Charles was permitted entrance into America. It was impossible for him to raise a fork or spoon of food to his mouth with his left hand so he fed himself totally with his right hand. He had no other trouble with the arm in any other way as he could handle it very well, but he was always very self-conscious about it when he sat down to a meal with strangers. Charles had been raised by two stepmothers, the first being his own mother's sister. Both his mother and first stepmother died very young. Charles, too, kept in touch with his family down through the years.

Almost from the very beginning of their marriage, English was spoken almost entirely in the home. Emma could understand the Flemish that Charles spoke fairly well, but could not reply in that language and vice-versa for Charles and Walloon. In mother's words, it was very comical, "We had a lot of laughs because of this," they both were to say many times down through the years.

Another source of amusement to both Charles and Emma, and a story that was told to the children many times, was when Emma discovered two weeks after they were married that Charles' thick, black hair was no longer black, but was already iron gray, at twenty-five years of age. He had been using hair black on it. Prematurely gray hair was a trait of the Vyvey family for centuries. Their hair was jet black when young, and turned gray at a very early age.

Charles and Emma subscribed to a Belgium newspaper printed in Flemish in Detroit, Michigan, and to the Vyvey-Verplancke children, it was always referred to as the "Belgium Paper" and it was NOT to be lost, handled or played with until Emma and Charles had read it thoroughly. They looked forward to its arrival each month with great anticipation. It held very little interest to the children who could not read it anyway. This publication was a part of the Vyvey family until

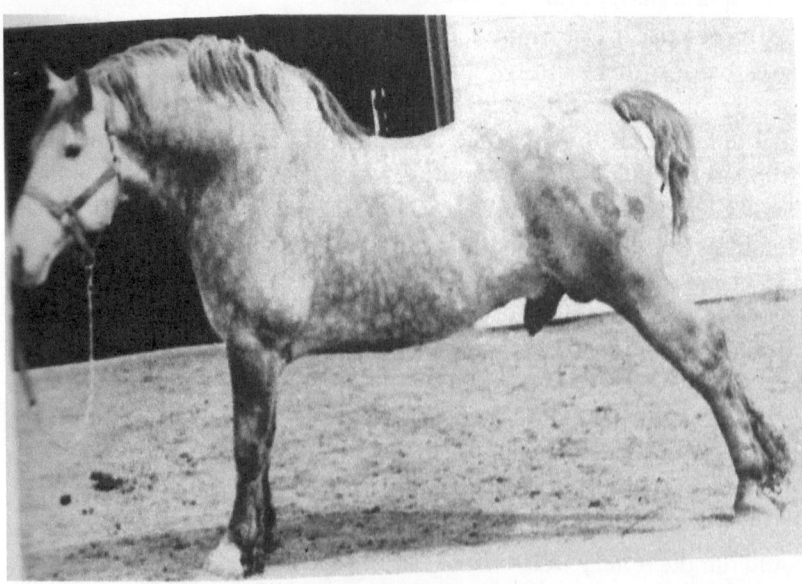

Mark, the original Belgian stud.

the 1950's when it was no longer published.

So it was that Charles and Emma began the building of a new home on Charles' homestead across Antelope Creek on the hillside some 100 yards from the Verplancke homestead. It, too, was built of logs but was two stories high with large bedrooms and a storeroom upstairs, living room and large dining room, kitchen, milk and storage rooms downstairs, and a full-length porch across the front. Years, later, a sun porch-bedroom was added to the east side.

Charles was known for his raising and handling of horses. The Belgian draft horses were his pride and joy! In the Belgium paper, Charles read of a Belgian stallion for sale in Iowa. Charles knew the people who raised these fine animals in Belgium and the stallion, Mark, was purchased and brought to the homestead and draft horses were then raised and sold in the valley. They were also sold to the tie camps in the area to be used as skid horses to skid the cut logs out of the mountains to the tie camps.

Another barn was built next to the first barn and totally enclosed corrals were built with huge doors as the entrance to the corral. The windmill and well house, which were attached to the house, became a nuisance to Emma with its clankety-clankety night and day so near the house. It was moved to a new location in the farther end of the corral and a long water trough to water the stock was built nearby. The children were schooled very early that the well house and windmill were off-limits to them. They were not playthings and were a strict "No-No" in every sense of the word.

In September 1912, Charles Louis Vyvey, Jr., nicknamed Carl, was born. The second son, John Lee, was born in October 1913. The estate of Peter Verplancke was still not settled at this time. So, the court appointed Charles Vyvey to be the administrator of the estate at Emma's request since he spoke English somewhat better than she.

It was a very tangled mess and creditors were still everywhere. It was decided by the court to put the Verplancke holdings up for sale to the highest bidder in the fall of 1914. Emma and Charles borrowed money and also made a bid on that day and got the place once again. She was fortunate that she had, of course, been awarded 160 acres of land of the place through the Homestead Act as a widow's share in the event of death. The creditors were paid by the court and the estate was finally settled in 1915, six years after Peter's death.

Emma and Charles both took up more homestead land, bringing the total size of the place in 1912 to 1260 acres of sagebrush homestead land. Eventually, after some 20 years, through acquisitions of nearby homesteads, and Bureau of Land Management properties, the place was to be a total of 3460 acres deeded land, most of which was cleared of the sagebrush and under cultivation.

The new house on Charles' homestead was nearly finished when they moved into it with the seven children. A huge granary, cow barn, corral, chicken house, woodshed, sawmill to cut the wood for the stoves, and a smokehouse and cellar were added to the buildings of the Vyvey place across the creek from the Verplancke place. A footbridge was built across this creek connecting the two places as one large cluster of buildings. Two more sons were added to the family, Albert Leopold, nicknamed Bert, was born in December 1914, and René Amé in July 1916.

Charles had applied for United States Citizenship. At his first examination to be naturalized, he was unable to remember the baby's name, René, and had to wait a full year for the next examination to be held. He became a naturalized citizen of the United States on October 10, 1917. When Charles and Emma would tell their children about this, it was always a source of amusement to the family and Charles was teased unmercifully about it. He got the most enjoyment of all out of it, though, and laughed harder than anyone else.

VI

Catastrophes

The storm clouds that were hanging over Europe erupted into World War I in 1917. With deep concern, Charles and Emma perused all the news available to follow the course of events of the conflagration. The sons of neighbors and friends were enlisting and going off to war. Belgium, of course, became a battlefield and soon was overcome and dominated by the enemy, Germany.

The horror of learning of the German use of poisonous gas at Hill Sixty and Ypres on the Canadian troops killing 5000 soldiers was unbelievable. Belgium was a great battlefield for the duration of the conflict, and then Flanders became a cemetery for those who had fallen there. The fields of red, red poppies and white crosses still mark the site of the heaviest fighting in their homeland.

Charles and Emma heard not a word from their loved ones for several years after World War I. Then, it was learned from Leo Hillewaert, who went back to Belgium for a year in the twenties, that Emma's family had been killed in the canal near their home by the Germans as they tried to flee into Holland. It was also at that time that Charles learned his family had survived and soon he was to receive letters from them again. From one of these letters, he learned that the gun, Big Bertha, as it was dubbed, had been mounted by the Germans between the outbuildings and the barn that was attached to the house where he was born. It was fired across the English Channel only twice and fell short of its target, England, both times. The second firing ripped it from its moorings and destroyed part of the barn and pig pens. Many of the animals were either killed or had to be destroyed. Big Bertha was dismantled many years later; only the cement block upon which it was mounted remains.

In 1918, Emma fell victim to the great flu epidemic that was sweeping the country. Many in the valley also were afflicted, and death swept through the isolated tie camps on French Creek and other areas. Volunteers, among them Charles, went to the tie camps and brought out the dead for burial. Several bodies at a time were brought out on sleds that winter.

Emma was very ill and everyone feared for her life. Gradually, however, she regained her strength and survival was won. The rest of the family miraculously escaped contracting the flu. Emma, however, was to have a side effect from this malady, it was discovered. It was a glandular imbalance, and she started gaining weight rapidly and consistently. Within two years her weight had nearly doubled and was from then on to fluctuate between 165 and 185 pounds. Her wit and good humor were to overcome this inconvenience, however.

In March, 1919, Charles and Emma welcomed their first daughter, Vivian Ruth to the family. She was a tiny baby with coal black hair and blue eyes. She was very fragile and was moved about on a pillow. It was discovered early in her life that she would never walk as she was paralyzed from the waist down. Near the end of her first year, she caught a cold which turned into pneumonia. She passed away in her mothers' arms in the old rocking chair, twenty-four hours before her first birthday.

The day of the funeral, her casket was placed in the back of the buggy. Charles and Emma rode up front and her older brothers rode behind in the back of the buggy. The funeral service was in the Beaver Creek schoolhouse. Neighbor girls were the pallbearers and the Rev. Clough[1] officiated at the services with Swan Olson and Wilbur Toothaker singing the hymns. Vivian was buried in the little country cemetery on the hill of the Platt Ranch.

One month later, a second daughter was born to Charles and Emma. In April 1920, Grace Carol joined the Vyvey family. I am that daughter and was destined to be the last living daughter in the Vyvey family. In October of 1921, another son, Arthur Warren, was born and was Number Twelve in Emma's family. When asked about his nickname, (Fox), mother would always say, "He was such a *foxy* little guy."

This, then, was to be the family of Verplancke-Vyvey – five Verplancke, children, two boys and three girls, and seven Vyvey children, five boys and two girls. We were raised as one family by Charles and Emma Vyvey.

---

[1] C.W. Clough, see *Saratoga Sun*, Mar. 18, 1920.

Many years later when I was 15 years old, and had learned to drive a car, mother and I would drive into Encampment together for mail, supplies and groceries. We would visit a lot and talk to each other coming and going as mother and daughter will do. Once, I remember she told me as we were chatting, how very homesick she was for Belgium when she first came to America. She said simply, "I would have swam the ocean to go home once if I could." I was deeply touched by her words and I said, "Mom, have you ever thought about the fact that here on Antelope Creek you have created your very own League of Nations? Very few can lay acclaim to a record in life like that."

She looked as me askance and asked what I meant by that? Hesitating for fear she would think me quite daft, I replied, "Mom, you have seven sons and their names tell the story better than anything anyone can ever say. They are named for Uncle Sam, five kings and one French president. Your oldest son is Sam for "Uncle Sam", and the kings are Charles, John, William, Albert and Arthur and the French President, René. Wasn't that what you had in mind?" She cracked up and laughed uproariously, but not to be outdone, she told me, "And you were named after the horse in the yard! The older kids couldn't agree on a name for you and to stop their bickering between the names Hattie and Maggie, I suggested we settle the argument and name you after the white horse in the yard. It stuck and you were named Grace." Each time we glanced at each other the rest of the way into town, we broke into laughter and occasionally, she would chuckle to herself.

The Verplanckes

Lucien Peter
(Sam)

Alice

Helena
(Lena)

Lillian

William
(Butch)

The Vyveys

Charles Jr.
(Carl)

John

Albert
(Bert)

René

Grace

Arthur
(Fox)

VII
Smokehouse and Cellar

The small smokehouse and cellar near the house was a very busy and vital place those first fifteen years after mother and dad moved into their home on the Vyvey homestead. Root vegetables from the garden were stored in the cellar after the fall harvest. Each kind and size had its own bin.

The smokehouse was a small building built of logs and the cellar was reached directly through a back door in that building. A huge, black, cast iron vat mounted on a cement firebox stood to the right of the doorway and two large sturdy butcher tables were in the middle of the room. It was here that the freshly butchered animals were cut up and readied for consumption by the family. Both mother and dad were adept at handling and cutting the meat. The hams and bacon were cured here. The fat from the butchered hogs was cut into two inch cubes and placed in the vat over the fire and rendered down into pure white lard and placed in containers. Always, after the lard was rendered, there remained the cracklings or rinds of the fat and skin of the animals in the bottom of the vat.

Generally, the next day or so, mother would return to the smokehouse and proceed with the last chore pertaining to usable portions of the butchered animal – the making of soap. Mother would do this alone and no children were to be in the building to distract her attention or risk being burned by the lye that was used on the cracklings in the vat. She stirred the hot boiling mass with a big wooden paddle that had a long handle so she would not be too close to the heat and fumes.

It seems to me that almost every part of the hog was prepared for use on the table in this building. The head was thoroughly debristled and cleaned and quartered with an axe. It was then boiled until the meat fell away from the bone. The meat was then chopped or ground, salt and pepper were added along with enough of the liquid to make it a pourable mass. It was then placed in loaf pans to cool. This 'head cheese' was served with hot mustard[1] on homemade bread. These sandwiches in our lunch boxes at school were the highlight of our school day. It didn't last long with five or six children in school at the same time.

The Belgian blood sausage was another family favorite. A cup of fresh pork blood was added to five pounds of seasoned sausage. This mixture was put into cleaned, pig casings and twisted ever so far. It was then boiled and hung to dry in the cellar. Fried apples, hot biscuits and fried blood sausage were a breakfast we eagerly ate. One of dad's favorites was scrambled eggs and brains and mother always saw to it that he had a nice portion of the small amount available after butchering.

In the early spring when the dandelions were in first bloom, we would go to the fields and pick fresh blossoms very carefully for mother to make her once-a-year dandelion wine. Both mother and dad enjoyed a glass of wine every day of their lives. I shall never forget the last batch of dandelion wine mother ever made. I do not know very much about winemaking, but what I do recall, I will tell you. The dandelion blossoms, orange slices, lemon slices, sugar, water and whatever else were put in, was always placed in a fifteen gallon crock and covered with cheesecloth. The crock was set in the smokehouse to ferment and ripen into wine.

Somehow, one of the hogs got out the pigpen and in her inquisitive freedom went to the smokehouse. Whether the door was ajar, or she managed to unhook the latch on the door, we will never know. However, she went inside and started lapping up the wine. All of a sudden, we all heard a terrible noise and the sow came out of that cellar with cheesecloth trailing behind her, staggering, reeling and squealing like we had never before heard. She was falling down, running and stopping now and then to sit down on her haunches and would shake her head rapidly back and forth. Mother was screaming to get her back into the pigpen. As the sow ran by the open barn door, she slithered inside and ran under some horses tethered in their stalls, all the while

---

[1] 2 tablespoons flour, 2 tablespoons dry mustard, 2 teaspoons sugar, 1 teaspoon salt. Mix these ingredients together into a thick paste. Thin with a little vinegar. It's hot.

squealing that awful squeal. Evidently, she got too near a horse who kicked her onto her rear and she came spinning out the barn door, landing on her rump. She sat there shaking her head as if to clear it. She gazed at the audience we made and quietly got up and headed for home – the pigpen. The sow was all right but mother was very upset about the broken crock and the loss of her wine. Mother never again made wine to my knowledge nor did she think the episode had any funny aspects as we children did.

VIII The Potato Patch and Mother's Garden

Every spring the children gathered in the cellar, each with a knife, and tackled the job of cutting the potatoes for planting the season's crop. Each child was shown how and where to cut the potatoes so each piece had an eye or two on it for the new shoots to start. After enough were cut, they were taken to the grainery and there, the older boys and dad would treat them with a formaldehyde solution to reduce the chance of the new potatoes developing a disease, such as dry rot, and losing part of the crop.

The potato patch was always in the field and quite large, covering several acres. The potato crop was indeed very vital, since the excess beyond the family's need was each year the barter for the food and clothing for the family.

A heavy frost which would kill the young plants was always feared. However, barring this frost and through very careful irrigating, the potatoes reached maturity in the fall. The children once again were assembled in the "tator patch," this time to pick and sack the potatoes in numerous gunnysacks. Dad would plow the potatoes up with a walking plow and team of horses, row after row. We would each take a row and pick up the potatoes by hand and then into the gunnysacks they went. Of course, there was always the competition game played by all. Who could pick a row the quickest? Whose bucket was filled first? And, who got the most sacks filled first? And just who could pick a full row without stopping for a rest? It was a tiring job as one was on one's hands and knees row after row, but the games helped immensely.

And so, the potatoes were sent to market in their gunnysacks sewed shut with the curved sack needle and binder twine with the two lovely ears made on each side during the sewing. What a joy when the potatoes were harvested, taken to market, and the pantry and storeroom were again stocked with winter staples and each one of the family had some new clothes and shoes for school and the cold of winter. I remember the boys' Rockford socks and canvas work gloves that were always bought by the dozen and mother's aprons and Mother-Hubbard dresses were there also.[1]

Then, there was mother's garden. Yes, it was mother's garden and was the talk of all around. The menfolk plowed, harrowed and leveled ground for her and from then on, it was mother's garden. She took the hoe and rake and made the long straight rows, planted the seeds, set out the plants and irrigated it herself. From the small narrow ditch of water provided by the reservoir for the garden (it was always called the garden ditch by the family) mother raised all kinds of vegetables: peas, beans, corn, carrots, beets, cabbage, cauliflower, celery, onions, radishes, lettuce, pumpkins, squash, cucumbers, Swiss chard and always she had three or four long rows of fresh flowers. I recall mainly the row of sweet peas, three to four feet tall and millions of beautiful sweet peas, so large and fragrant. She always gave her neighbors who came to call beautiful huge bouquets and they always wound up "ooing" and "ahing" over her garden and flowers. The currant and gooseberry bushes were near the house and I have no idea how many milk pails of currants my youngest brother, Fox and I picked for the currant jelly mother made. Picking the currants was always a game of competition, also. Who could pick the fastest, the most, the cleanest with no leaves or stems in the berries? The reward was always the same – whether picking berries or picking potatoes – the sense of accomplishment. The job was finished and it wasn't that bad after all.

In the late summer the older boys would ride horses up to the mountains and pick chokecherries and come home with sacks of the berries across their laps. Mother made quarts and quarts of chokecherry syrup for the pancakes and biscuits we had for our winter breakfasts along with eggs or bacon. Now, in our later years, as my bothers and I reminisce about those depression years and our childhood, we always wind up agreeing that none of us can ever remember a time when we were hungry or cold.

---

[1] EDITORS NOTE: Grace as a young girl always wore a calf-length dress and dark stockings. As the weather became colder, Grace would merely wear more dresses, as many as four or five at a time. She wore her dark, wavy hair long until one day at school when her teacher bobbed it short. When Emma saw what had happened to Grace's beautiful long hair, she was extremely angry!

We all had the same problem speaking two languages that were quite mixed up until we were well into school and finally speaking only English. There has been and always will be a deep closeness and a bond in Charles and Emma's family that will remain until we are all gone from this earth. Love, deep concern and respect for each other and the Vyvey-Verplancke family seem to be the roots our parents sought for each of us.

IX
Badges of Courage

Each morning mother appeared in the kitchen wearing a coverall apron. Very, very seldom was mother without her apron. The pockets held things needed immediately and were always at her fingertips. Safety pins, buttons, a pencil, a hairpin, or whatever, always appeared out of her apron pocket. Letters in the country mailbox always went into her apron after a quick scrutiny to be perused later when a few minutes were available for rest and quiet, as she referred to those times.

Mother loved the chore of peeling potatoes. It was one thing she never wanted any help with as she said, "It is one of the few things I can do in the kitchen while sitting down and resting." The apron also had a place in the preparation of potatoes. She would fold the bottom of her apron to form a bag, place just the right amount of potatoes for the day's meals there and carry them to her favorite chair and table to do the peeling. The same held true for apples, vegetables and fruits for canning or pies. This time, too, was generally a time of her telling me many of the things I am writing about now. The bread she would make was very well known to friends and neighbors as well as the family. To this day, I've had many old-timers from the valley, say to me, "I shall never forget your mother's bread and the smell of that bread while it was baking in the house."

The first thing mother taught me to make when I was old enough to learn to help with the cooking was white bread. I did not learn to make one or two loaves but fourteen loaves and a pan of 48 rolls for dinner. It took until well into the afternoon for the loaves of bread to be baked and cooled for eating. We baked bread every fifth day and the kneading was the biggest and hardest chore for me. That was an awful lot of dough to handle. Bread requires a lot of kneading to have a good texture and my arms would ache fiercely during this process. My biggest reward was the day she said, "Grace, your bread is as good as mine." I grew an inch right on the spot! The recipe was not in a cookbook or on a sheet of paper as mother's written English was very difficult to read. Any writing to be done for mother and dad would be generally left to the children. The Belgian writing of letters was of a different composition than our Palmer method and much more detailed. They both wrote the same script with the strange loops and slants. Ours was just as strange to them, and they always liked the typed letters best.

To get back to the bread recipe, and any other recipe I was taught, it was always given to me in the same fashion – so many sifters of flour, a pinch or handful of salt, shortening the size of an egg or a walnut, a tablespoon of this, a teaspoon or two of that, a pinch of this, and the white pitcher always only of water or milk, grease the baking pans, check the oven temperature, add more wood to the fire or wait awhile and don't hurry anything! The secret of texture of any baking was time and mixing.

After I had mastered the art of making the bread from memory, I went to making the pies for the family – always three or four at a time – and then on to preparing the salads or green vegetables. There was washing and cleaning of the lettuce, radishes and onions from the garden for the table. These were the duties turned over to me. Yes, when I married and had only the two of us to cook for, I had to use all my ingenuity and common sense to come up with the right amount of anything. I learned, though, and the reward was when my husband would say, "Gee, this tastes like your mother's."

Next to mother's apron, her second badge of courage was her broom. All her family remembers mother and her broom and the impact it made on our lives. It was a source of laughter, of discipline and of her courage to settle any conflict that arose. During my early years, the highway from Riverside to Walden was not where it is today as it passed the ranch. It traveled a mile along the top of the hill east of the house and ranch buildings, down a lane for a mile, over Beaver Creek and up the hill above the Platt ranch.

Beaver Creek and the lane were always an overnight stopping place for the gypsies who traveled the road during the spring and early fall of each year. They would annoy the Platt family as well as our family. Generally, dad and the older boys would be in the fields when the gypsies would appear afoot at the top of the hill near the house. They were spotted immediately by one of the family as they came down the hill toward the buildings and the shout, "Mom, here come the gypsies" issued the warning. Quickly, we were told to stay put in the house and mother would grab her broom and dash out the door, straight toward them. They always separated a bit and as we peeked out the windows, they were quite a sight to see – bright colored, billowy skirts flapping in the wind clear down to their ankles, flowered blouses with full sleeves, the kerchiefs tied in gypsy fashion, and jewelry and huge earrings such as we had never seen. There stood mother in her apron, brandishing her broom to give a determined emphasis to her command to go back to their camp and leave her chickens, her garden, and anything else that met their fancies, strictly alone. We often wondered if they understood mother's brogue any better than she did theirs, or if it was her broom that convinced them they were not welcome to pilfer anything and hide it in their bright colored billowy clothes. As they would turn and go back up the hill to their camp for the night, old Shep, the watchdog, was left on guard all night. The next morning the gypsy camp would be gone to greener pastures.

The broom also served as the alarm clock for us upstairs. Mother would rap on the ceiling underneath our beds quite sharply with the end of the handle, which meant GET UP! The broom was always the symbol that meant business. Occasionally, at bedtime, the boys would resort to scuffling and wrestling with one another and generally became noisy and rowdy in their bedrooms before going to sleep at night. If it continued after an admonition was shouted up the stairway for quiet and bedtime, up the stairs would come mother with the broom in her hand. Her appearance in the bedroom doorway was all it took. Peace and quiet reigned from that moment on and day was done.

As long as I can remember, my dad carried a pocket knife in his trouser pocket along with a piece of chewing tobacco. He also carried a pocket watch with a leather thong attached. The thong was slit in the other end, which served as a buttonhole so it could be buttoned to one of the buttons on top of his trouser that also held his wide suspenders in place. Occasionally, he would stop whatever he was doing and reach for his pocketknife and plug of tobacco and cut a small piece and begin chewing. Mother would always reprimand him if some of the juice from the tobacco would dribble down his chin. Eventually, he quit chewing altogether. He enjoyed his pipe and a good smoke during his leisure hours, particularly after supper in the evening. From time to time, he would get upset if he couldn't find his pipe where he had left

it as he never carried it with him. All the children, however, found it to be the best available instrument to blow soap bubbles all over the yard.

The pocket knife was always available to repair this or that as the occasion arose. He would whittle plugs for oil and grease pans or kerosene cans that came up with their caps missing. If a harness for the horses needed repairing, out would come the pocket knife. He would cut a new strap and make a hole with the nice leather punch, so it could be laced with leather thongs which he had cut in long strips. After supper in the wintertime, dad would get out the shoe last with its many sized lathes, a sizeable piece of raw leather, small shoe hammer, tiny shoe nails, and the pocket knife. He would cut the soles for the various shoes in the family with the pocket knife. Always, he placed a substantial amount of the tiny nails in his mouth and, one by one, he would take them and nail the soles to the shoes. The iron last the shoe was slipped onto would bend the points of the nails as they touched it. Each nail received an extra sound tap so no tip of the nail could poke into the foot when the shoe was on the wearer. Then, the shoe was slipped off the last and with his pocket knife, he very carefully trimmed the leather around the shoe.

The pocket knife was the main instrument dad used for the toys he made for the children. He made whistles for us out of the green willow branches in the spring after they were filled with sap so the bark would slip off easily when tapped gently. He would cut the main notch and the blower slot very carefully with the knife, slip the bark back on, and we had our whistle. The toy we prized the most was the one he made with the hazelnut and small potato. Using the ever present pocket knife, he would take a leather punch blade and bore three holes in the hazelnut, one in each end and a small one in a side of the nut. Carefully, he would remove the inside meat out of these holes with a sharp-pointed awl or needle. Next, he whittled a stick about six inches long, round and slender with a little wider top and a sharp point on the bottom. Taking a piece of heavy cord, he tied it securely to the stick, some three quarters of the way up from the pointed end. He threaded the string through the side holes in the hazelnut, then tied a loop in the end of the string to fit one's finger. Slipping the stick down through the tip and bottom holes made in the nut, it was aligned so that the string tied to the stick came out the side hole straight. A small potato was stuck securely on the pointed end of the stick for balance. Winding up the string tautly with the top of the stick and pulling it at a good clip, it would spin the potato faster and faster, back and forth and rewind itself up around the stick in yo-yo fashion. It fascinated the children.

Dad loved the games of checkers, Chinese checkers and the card game of Solo. Therefore, every evening, during the winter months, these three games were played simultaneously by the family. They were alternated nightly as to choice and all played all three very well. Competition would be keen and bickering of any kind was quickly squelched and playing continued.

Dad was the Treasurer of School District No. Ten for some eighteen years, which was an added challenge. Each time he went to the school board election, he would tell mother he would refuse to take the responsibility another time. He would come home, sheepishly carrying the books each time. Finally, he hit upon the solution of having the books kept up to date all the time. I was the solution. He took me to his big desk and explained what was expected and how it was to be done. After all the entries in income and expenditures were posted in their proper columns, they were to balance properly or there was an error. This was my first lesson in bookkeeping, and evidently the reason I continued to work as a bookkeeper throughout my life. Each year that he would come home from the Carbon County Superintendent of School's office, after the audit of the books, he would smile and tell me they had been pleased with the books. It was a pleasant and rewarding accomplishment we shared.

X   Broken Bones and Bloody Noses

It is a wonder to my brothers and me that there were so few serious accidents or a tragedy of some kind to overtake one of us as we were growing up. Most of our antics to wear out our energy, both at work and at play, were quite unorthodox and were usually dreamed up on the spur of the moment and were invariably motivated by competition.

There was a buck-and-rail fence leading from the house up the steep hill to the crest of the hill east of the house. The last couple hundred feet was very steep and the top pole of the fence seemed even steeper. It was quite a sight, I am sure, to see six or seven children walking the top pole, balancing only with our arms and surefootedness. The steep incline was a trial and it took many attempts to conquer, but we all, at one time or another, accomplished this feat. Then, we would run to ask mom and dad to watch us do it. No way would mother watch us, as she was sure one of us would get hurt. Instead, she would tell us she was raising children and that we looked like magpies around the place that were learning to fly, especially with our arms waving and our feet trying to clutch the pole. I am sure she watched from the window with her heart in her throat. Dad would just grin and say, "It's fun, isn't it?"

During the summer months, when the evenings were long and cool, the boys held their own rodeos in the cow corral, riding the bucking skim-milkers, bull-dogging the cows and generally getting bucked off and thrown into the fence. I don't know who won the contest – the animals or the boys. From my vantage point as spectator, I would say it was a toss-up. We always had fun at whatever we did, whether it was sledding, tobogganing, skiing, skating or the wiener roasts and taffy pulls.

Helena, or Lena as she was known, was indeed an outdoor girl and was very good with breaking horses and helping with the outdoor work about the place. She was fearless and obstinate when it came to riding an unbroken horse. She would be thrown off time and again and always would get up and try again until she won and the horse was completely subdued.

Once, she saved her brother Sam's life with her dexterity and quick-thinking as they were rounding up horses for branding one day. Dad and Carl were witnesses to this feat. As they were galloping and chasing the animals, Sam's saddle suddenly turned, dropping them both underneath the horse. His foot was caught in the stirrup of the saddle when the horse got up and started running and kicking at the saddle and Sam. Sam somehow got hold of the horse's kicking leg with both arms and held on. Lena saw what was happening and, not being able to get close enough to the kicking and running horse to grab the reins and bring him to a halt, she grabbed her lariat and roped the running horse. She then snubbed him close to the saddle horn on her horse. She got her pocketknife out and cut the cinch to Sam's saddle in two. He was free of the horse and danger, but not free of the saddle. His foot had gone clear through the stirrup and they had to saw it in two to free him. His ability to hang on to the leg of the kicking and running horse and Lena's quick thinking had most assuredly saved his life. He had been kicked several times and was bruised, bleeding, and badly scratched, but he had no broken bones. He was fully conscious when rescued.

Shortly thereafter, he continued his work with the horses. Had he not been strong enough to hold on to the horse's kicking foot, he surely would have been drug to death as this hold kept the horse unbalanced and deterred his ability to kick and run as a horse is capable of doing when unhindered.

My youngest brother, Fox, and I had two narrow escapes from death together when we were both very young. Neither of us was aware of the danger when it happened.

I was about twelve and he nearly eleven when the first took place. One fall day we were walking home from school, side by side, and as was our inclination from time to time, we decided to cut across the neighbor's meadow and cutting off about a half mile of walking instead of following the road which was fenced with barbed wire on both sides down the lane to home. Swinging our lunch pails and chattering all the while, we both heard a terrible thumping and yelling behind us. Glancing back over our shoulders, we recognized the danger at once and obeyed immediately the command to run for the fence as hard as we could. The neighbor's huge bull with the long pointed and upturned horns was pounding straight for us. The neighbor on horseback was trying to avert the bull by riding into him with his horse and knocking him down or away from us. We ran as hard as we could and scrambled through the barbed wire fence, tearing our hands on the barbs of the wire, and then we ran for the bridge. The neighbor and his horse managed to turn the bull not more than twenty-five feet away from us.

The neighbor rode up to us and told us never to cross the meadow again, which we didn't. We never saw the animal in the meadow again and never knew from whence the neighbor came and saw what was about to happen or how far he had been attempting to turn the bull by running into him with the horse. The meadow was at least a quarter mile by a quarter mile and we had cut across it diagonally. I don't recall either of us saying a word as we hurried home.

The next close call we had was when I was fifteen and Fox was nearly fourteen. We were on our way to school, each riding our horse. It was January and the temperature at 54° below zero that morning. I believe it was the coldest recorded temperature on Beaver Creek at that time. There was no wind and in the stillness the squeak of our horses' hooves on the hard icy road carried quite a distance.

We rode side by side at a gentle trot, not speaking, but listening to the sound that the even gait made in the stillness of that morning. We came to a wooden bridge half way down the lane, and as our horses' feet hit the icy bridge, they both lost their footing. My horse and I hit the bridge first, and Fox and his horse fell on top of us. Fox and his horse scrambled to their feet and Fox was not hurt. My horse scrambled to its feet and then Fox saw that I was not moving and that my foot was caught in the stirrup of the saddle. My horse had always been a little skittish so Fox inched his way to her. He found she stood perfectly still while he extricated my foot from the stirrup. She made no effort to run. I was unconscious and knew nothing of what was going on. A brief moment of clarity hit me, and as one in a dream, I saw Fox lead the horse and tie her to the fence. After Fox tied my horse up and thinking I was done for, he jumped on his horse and ran home for help.

When dad and brother John got to the top of the hill the sight they saw astounded them. Somehow, I had gotten up in my unconsciousness and walked to my horse, untied and mounted her. She was running at a full gallop, taking me home. They could tell something was terribly wrong from the way I was riding, nearly falling off one side and then the other. They stopped as I got closer and John ran to stop my horse, removed me from the saddle gently and took me home. I regained consciousness late the next afternoon and had no broken bones or bruises, just the loss of a day and a half in my time.

Dad had a very harrowing and frightening experience one summer evening during irrigating season. It, too, was totally unexpected with no warning. During irrigating time the days are quite long for the irrigator. They go to change their water at four o'clock in the morning, and again during the day, and once again late in the evening after supper.

This particular evening after supper, Dad mounted his horse, Prince, that he had ridden for a number of years and rode to the patch of oats he was irrigating at the far north end of the ranch near the highway to Walden. His horse was well trained and by dropping the reins to the ground, Prince would stay put wherever he was left. This was the case this evening.

Dad walked away with the shovel and began changing some of the water to a high spot in the grain that the water was not getting to. Absorbed in his work shoveling out a small ditch for the water to fall to the high spot, he was totally unaware of the danger he was within moments to encounter. His horse emitted a strange snort, and looking up at him, dad saw the fright in the animal and only the tips of the reins were touching the ground as he held his head high and snorted again. Turning and looking the direction the horse was looking, dad saw a sight he was never able to forget nor the fright he felt at that moment. There, in front of him, stood a huge bear on his hind legs, mouth wide-open and coming straight for dad. To my knowledge, it was the only bear ever seen on the ranch itself. There were bear in the mountains, yes, but never down on the ranch. Dad's only chance, he felt, was to get to his horse and run, for his shovel was little protection against an animal such as this. He started for the horse carefully, the bear following and grunting now and then. The horse was slowly backing away from them both, reins still tipping at the ground. The horse snorted loudly and backed away and dad, being a little closer, leaped at the same time and grabbed the reins. He mounted the moving horse quickly and after settling him down, looked to see where the bear was. Evidently, the loud snorting of the horse and the quick, unexpected movement of dad, spooked the bear for it had dropped to all four feet and was lumbering off toward the highway. Later, a young married couple reported that the bear crossed the highway in front of their car and had two little cubs following her.

Each of the children had various accidents, which resulted in a few broken bones, bruises, scratches, and bloody noses at some time or another, of course, as all families have. Brother René had a quick and unexpected skirmish with a frisky, young colt one morning. René and Bert were in the corral where a mare and her colt were. As René passed behind the young colt, he grabbed the colt's tail and gave it a flip. The colt kicked high and true and hit René on the chin, laying it wide open and knocking him to the ground. As the boys came to the house, blood was soaking René's shirt and numerous stitches were needed to close the wound. He carries a deep scar around the bottom of his chin from this encounter.

John and Carl were the only ones to receive broken bones. John broke his wrist riding a toboggan over a jump built in the snow on the steep hill next to the house. He and the toboggan parted company high in the air and he landed on his hands, breaking one wrist. Carl broke a leg while doing some roping when working cattle. The rope got under the fender on the saddle and a quick jerk by the animal at the end of the rope, snapped his leg bone. He was laid up several weeks. In another accident, he dislocated a hip. The doctor was called to the ranch. Carl was laid on the floor in the living room and by the light of the kerosene lamp, the doctor saturated a cloth with chloroform, administered it to Carl and snapped the hip back into place. But, they couldn't revive Carl. The doctor was sure the bad light had contributed to the overdose of chloroform. Dad and the doctor worked over an hour and a half to bring him around. Once again, all was well.

Mother also had some freakish and serious accidents. She loved to fish, and nearly every afternoon in the summer she would get her willow pole and line with a .22 caliber shell for a sinker and fish awhile in the stream near the house. Her usual catch was several eight-to-ten inch brook trout. We were all sure mother could catch fish where no one else ever could. Her blue eyes would twinkle and she would laugh so hard when we would tell her this.

The biggest fish she ever caught was a five and a half pound Rainbow from one of dad's fishponds on the ranch. She held tight to the willow pole as she ran up the incline dragging the fish out of the pond behind her. Was she ever proud of that fish! We all were.

When mother was preparing to go fishing one day, she got a good-sized hook caught deep in the flesh of one upper arm. The force of whatever happened buried the hook beyond the barb. She was taken to the doctor. As the hook was so close to an artery, he had to cut the eye from the shank of the hook and pull the barbed point clear through her arm. Nearly the same thing happened to her one day in a different way.

Emma and her 5 1/2 pound rainbow.

She was in the grainery helping dad and the boys sack several tons of oats they had sold. As the gunnysacks were filled, she did the sewing up of the sacks with two ears on either side with binder twine and a long curved sack needle. With the force of pulling the needle through a couple of layers of the gunnysack to make an ear on one side, her hands slipped and it plunged the needle deep into one arm. This time an artery was punctured and she was rushed to the doctor. Again, all went well.

Around this time, dad paid $1.00 to the Big Creek Ranch for ten miles of phone line so that the ranch would have a telephone. It was the first telephone installed on Beaver Creek. Bert and Fox performed the duties of linemen, keeping the lines up and in working order through all kinds of weather. The neighbors all paid Bert and Fox $2.00 a month for the maintenance. The ladies on the line thrived with the new communication so available. One time, Mrs. Henry Flohr, in her anxiety to tell her friends and neighbors some news, cranked up her phone which supplied an adequate shock to Bert who was in the process of splicing the phone wire.

Other than colds and runny noses, the children were quite healthy. I only know of two communicable diseases we had in the home. One was the mumps, slight cases, and only a few members of the family had them. The other was the hard German measles. This was an entirely different story.

A neighbor family had the measles and had no country telephone. The nearest phone was ours and the oldest son of that family came to our house to use the telephone to call the doctor. They lived four or five miles from us and the boy was not feeling well himself as he was coming down with the measles, too. After his call and a short rest, he went home. We caught the measles a week or ten days later.

At one point in the following month, mother had eight children down with the measles at the same time. Some of us were bedded downstairs in the living room and the four older ones in their beds upstairs. Our rooms were darkened to protect our eyes and during the high fevers, we were not allowed out of our beds. Poor mother! I will never know how she managed to make the dozens of trips up those stairs to care for and feed us bedridden up there. As we all broke out with the ugly red splotches and the fevers subsided, she knew we were all on the way to recovery except one. John was slow breaking out and the fever raged on and on. He had nosebleeds and spitting up of blood and remained sick for quite some time. After the measles were over, he was very weak and still ill all the time. Upon taking him to the doctor, it was discovered he had a bad case of yellow jaundice, hepatitis. None of the rest of the family caught it, but John ailed for several months and finally recovered completely. This period of our adolescence, I am sure, was the most trying for mother. She was so weary and her steps upstairs became slower and slower.

There were many other incidents that remain in my memory bank, and from time to time they surface and the family will discover them. Always these discussions begin with words, "Do you remember?" We all remember them very well and occasionally, the discussions become very heated as we all remember it in a different fashion as to the impression it made on us at the time or what part one of us played in the event.

Two such incidents, so serious, are always treated with much mirth and hilarity when discussed by the family during one of these "Do you remember?" sessions. Both of these incidents involved the youngest member of the family, Fox.

The first incident happened before Fox had started to school, so he was only about five or so at the time. One morning around 9:00 a.m., Fox came up missing and mother couldn't find him anywhere. When the older boys came to the house from the fields, they searched and searched, but no trace was found of him. Shortly after 11:00 a.m., dad left his chores in the field to return to the house for the noonday meal, totally unaware of the anxiety and growing apprehension that was consuming the family there. From time to time, as dad was coming up the road, he thought he heard a child cry out, and occasionally it sounded like a sobbing child. He saw nothing and put it down in his mind as imagination or thought his ears were playing tricks on him.

Continuing up the road, the cries grew louder and louder and more distinct. About a quarter mile from the house, he noticed the big gate ahead of him across the road was not in its usual closed position, but rather lying flat on the ground. The crying of a child grew louder and more distinct as he approached the gate, and then, he saw Fox. The big heavy eight-pole gate had Fox pinned to the ground and one pole lay across his chin. He had been pinned there for hours in the hot sun. As dad lifted the gate off him Fox informed dad very seriously that, "That damn gate sure is heavy, Daddy!" As we saw dad carrying him home, we all wondered where he found him. Fox had decided to go where his dad was in the field and having trouble opening the heavy gate, he climbed to the top. As he was going down the other side, it fell flat to the ground on top of him. His lips, cheeks and dimpled chin were bruised and swelling rapidly and the sunburn had turned him deep red. He was a sorry sight, but was not injured.

The second incident was also frightening and very hilarious at the same time. He was by far more articulate as his howling could be heard a mile or more away and he had quite an audience as several of the Big Creek ranch cowboys were at the ranch that evening with the trail herd they were taking to the railroad at the Canyon Ranch. They were spending the night at the ranch, which was halfway to their destination.

There was an old well in the yard near the house lined with a five foot or six foot cast casing. It had been abandoned some years before when a new well was drilled next to the front door of the house for the pump to be more accessible for domestic use. Fox was about seven or eight years old and for some reason known only to him, he decided to try the well on for size. He pointed one foot down the pipe and watched it go down about a foot, then started to draw back. His foot wouldn't budge. The heel and toe of his shoe were anchored solidly to the sides of the casing. Jumping around on the other leg and screaming at the top of his lungs, the Fox was caught. The audience quickly gathered around the trapped Fox and above all the din he was emitting, everyone was giving him advice on what to do to get

his foot out of the well. Perhaps he couldn't hear it, what with both his howls of consternation and the howls of laughter and advice from the cowboys and the family and mother and dad's concern of freeing him. I believe he listened to mother and dad and managed to pull his foot gently out of his shoe and thus was free of the thing. His foot was intact and they didn't have to saw his leg off as the cowboys had suggested during the fracas.

Probably the most serious experience while growing to adulthood for the family happened to the oldest son, Sam. While in their late teens and early twenties, the older boys in the family would occasionally, on a Saturday night, attend the dance being held in the Encampment City Hall. This particular Saturday night, three or four of my bothers attended the dance. During the evening, a commotion was heard at the front door of the dance hall.

The dancers stopped and crowded around the entrance to see what was happening. Backing away from the doorway, the crowd couldn't believe their eyes. With loud and abusive language, a stranger was trying to enter the dance hall astride his saddle horse. The Deputy Sheriff of Saratoga, Russell Baldwin, was attempting to convince him to stay outside with the horse or someone might get hurt. The rider refused to listen and managed to push past the sheriff into the hall on his horse. The sheriff asked Sam, who was near the door, to help him get the intruder out of the hall. Sam leaped forward, grabbed the reins of the horse with his left hand, and with his right hand, reached up to yank the rider out of the saddle to the floor. During this attempt, a swish of glistening steel was seen as either a knife or a straight razor used by the rider, slashed Sam's throat. He was bleeding profusely and was taken immediately from the dance hall to the garage across the street. Quickly, two mechanics on duty – Kels Nichols and "Barn" Tillou – made bandages using grease rags. They knotted the rags and tightly bandaged the open wound. "Barn" Tillou raced Sam to Doctor Beetle in Saratoga. As the doctor had been alerted, he was waiting for Sam in his office. Sam, feeling it was all over for him, gave his new coat to Carl before leaving. Carl raced home to the ranch to inform mother and dad.

Doctor Beetle gave Sam a swig of wine and without any other anesthetic, placed twenty-two stitches in his neck wound. The jugular artery was not cut, but was scratched and bruised. The doctor commended the two mechanics on their quick thinking in knotting the rags and bandaging Sam's throat.

Sam was kept in Saratoga several days where the doctor could give him the attention he needed. He has carried this long scar on this neck and throat all his life. The rider of the horse was given only a seven and a half month jail sentence.

Now, brother William had a mishap also. William, by the way was nicknamed Butch. At one point in time, Butch Cassidy and his gang of outlaws passed through the ranch and, like other travelers, stopped to eat with our family. Brother Sam saw a likeness between his brother, William, and Butch Cassidy, the outlaw. Sam, of course, began calling William "Butch" and the name stuck. Anyway, Butch's mishap occurred while trying to rope a horse they wanted to catch. The end of the rope was not anchored to the saddle horn of the horse he was riding at the time, but instead, wrapped around his own arm which could have been disastrous. When the horse he had roped hit the end of the rope, Butch was yanked from his horse by the rope wrapped around his arm and drug a quarter mile through the quaker patch above the reservoir before the rope came unwrapped from his arm. He was badly bruised and scratched from head to foot and ached in every bone of his body for a time. He was a sorry sight and a subdued young man who had learned a lesson the hard way and the making of a man took another step forward.

Many times great lessons are taught and never forgotten, even from the might-have-beens. After things are done in seeking adventure, they are thought about and remembered years and years later. While we are young, we think only of the play and fun they are at the time. One fun thing was riding the makeshift cart – two large wagon wheels held together only by an axle and nothing else – down the steep, steep hill east of the house. There were no brakes and nothing to guide it with except the shifting of your body. There was no way to get off but fall off, get thrown off, or fall off backward. It all seems a ridiculous thing now to do, much less dream up and actually try. No one was ever hurt doing this, but I still have no idea why it was ever tried or who started it.

In the teen years, boxing gloves appeared on the ranch.[1] Boxing, hand-wrestling and plain, old-fashioned wrestling were favorite sports among my brothers. No matter how hard the day's work had been, after the good hot delicious supper was over, there was always a boxing match or two or some wrestling matches to take care of their boundless energy on the long, summer evenings. The boxing

---

[1] Carl, also nicknamed Popcorn, took his boxing seriously and soon became a leading contender and the Platte Valley favorite.

matches produced black eyes, cuts, and many, many bloody noses and the wrestling produced pulled muscles, limps and sore spots that were quickly healed and forgotten. One time, brother John got into a boxing match with Ralph Platt, Jr. out in the barn at the Platt Ranch. When Ralph's mother, who was on her way to feed the pigs, found them, she admonished them to stop the boxing. When her repeated admonitions went unheeded, she stopped the match abruptly and both boys went home to wash off the pig slop.

These were a few of the events and probably the best remembered of the trials of the family growing to adulthood. It certainly was quiet around home at night. The days were filled with everything imaginable, but after retiring at night, there was total rest and quiet. The only sounds we knew at night, if we happened to lie awake awhile, were the wind, the patter of rain on the roof, the howling of coyotes in the fields, the bawling of the calves at weaning time, and the mooing of the cows to comfort them. Occasionally, the barking of the dog would wake us up when a coyote came too close or a skunk or weasel would try to steal a chicken or two from the hen house. We would awaken to the sound of a lone meadowlark, a woodpecker at work in the tree over the house, and magpies chattering and roosters crowing. The day would start anew and soon was filled with voices, laughter and chores to be done, school to attend and plenty of good food on the table.

The boys at play.

XI
Troubled 20's and Early 30's

    The years of the twenties were as hard and discouraging as the early years on the homestead except there were more hands and backs to help with the hard work about the place. Having lost all that had been gained in the preceding years when the stock market for cattle plunged to an all time low, once again, Charles and Emma started over. The steers, purchased with a loan from the bank for forty dollars a head, had been kept and fed for two years. After the market fell, Charles and Emma had to sell them for less than forty dollars a head. Dad went with the cattle on the train to Denver. After the sale of the steers, there was not enough money left over the loan at the bank for a train ticket home. Dad had to borrow money from a friend to get home.

    After all the necessary paper work was straightened out pertaining to the property, water rights and so forth, Charles and Emma's attorney helped them to apply for a federal loan to assist in getting them on their feet once again. When they received the letter informing them to come to the attorney's office in Rawlins to sign the necessary papers to receive the approved federal loan, they had not the funds to make the trip. The loan had to be forfeited. Shortly thereafter, a new loan was applied for with the State of Wyoming. This loan was also approved and met with success when all was signed, sealed, and delivered.

    During this period, more and more land was being cleared of sagebrush and grain crops of oats, barley and wheat were larger and larger. The ever present potato patch also thrived. Horses were still raised and sold in the valley and the herd of Hereford cattle was slowly, but surely, growing too.

About 1918, a strange machine came to the ranch. Mother and dad purchased a gasoline engine. It was a twelve horsepower, one cylinder, gas-powered engine to be used in the sawmill and to run the thrashing machine. It was with great incredulity that the family gathered around the strange machine when it was brought to the ranch.

Dad, with instructions in hand, set about getting it started. Not having the modern convenience of a battery-powered starter, a large flywheel had to be turned by hand in order to start it. After several unsuccessful tries, it finally sputtered into a great noisy chugging. As it erupted into action, the family fled every which way, running for their lives. Dad bravely sneaked up on the noisy monster, and instructions in hand, gingerly turned the choke on the bottom of the carburetor, causing it to sputter and die.

All was well and laughingly, the family came back to timidly inspect the first gasoline engine on Beaver Creek.

Some changes were also taking place in the family at this time. The middle daughter of the Verplancke family, Alice, was married in the early twenties and was living on a nearby farm. The other two Verplancke daughters, Helena and Lillian left home one Sunday morning on horseback, supposedly to attend Sunday school. They traveled in this fashion to Carbondale, Colorado, where they obtained work on a ranch.

The letters written home from them always found their way into mother's apron pocket, and she would read them to the children now and then. There was great excitement for the younger children when the small packages would come from them with little gifts on birthdays and Christmas for a year or two.

One evening a lone rider on horseback rode up to the kitchen door at the homestead. It was Helena. She took up a small homestead near the home place, built a small house of logs and a barn and lived there until she proved up on it. Shortly thereafter, she married and sold the homestead to mother and dad and she lived near or in Saratoga, Wyoming, the rest of her life.

Several months after Lena returned home, mother and dad received word that Lillian was in critical condition from a gunshot wound. Mother, dad, Helena and William left immediately to go to her bedside. The family at home was left in Carl's care until their return.

Leaving late in the afternoon, they traveled all night in a heavy downpour and over muddy roads to arrive early the next morning in Carbondale. They were too late, as Lillian had died a few hours before their arrival. The circumstances surrounding her death were very inconclusive as whether it was murder or suicide and the accounts from the newspapers that I have read about it, point out this fact very strongly. She was buried in Glenwood Springs, Colorado.

It was during this time that I became acquainted with that infernal churn. The duty of churning butter was handed down one-by-one as we became old enough to handle the huge churn. The same held true with the turning of the blower wheel to keep the coals hot in the forge in the blacksmith's shop. The forge was used to heat the plowshares for the plows so the shoes on them could be sharpened. It was also used to heat the horseshoes so they could be fitted for the horses or anything of metal that had to be sharpened or shaped. Dad and his sons did most of the blacksmith duties themselves.

Back to the churn! It was huge and half full of gallons and gallons of cream. Round and round, hour after hour, one turned that infernal churn with the handle at the side of its potbelly. The churn was held in place in its own stand so it could be turned, the cream going Slosh! First against the bottom and then Slosh! against the top as it was turned. Slish! Slosh! Slish! Slosh! For an eternity it seemed. Then, the joy of hearing it go Thump! Thud! Thump! Thud! And one knew it was turning into butter. Mother would pour a pitcher or two of very cold water into the churn and after a few more minutes of rapid turning, the butter would wash clean of buttermilk and gather in a huge batch of butter. She would remove the mass from the churn, wash it again and again with water, and work it all out with a wooden butter paddle, salt it just right and form it into one pound butter forms and wrap it in butter papers purchased at the store. Generally, each batch of butter would certainly yield eighteen to twenty pounds of butter and a sizeable amount of fresh buttermilk for the family. We all had our stint with the butter churn. We all hated the job because of its monotony and lack of variety or competition connected with the chore. It was just plain drudgery. You couldn't trade the job or give it away. No one wanted it, and you were left strictly alone while you turned and turned and turned.

A favorite around home was cottage cheese. Raw cow's milk was put through the separator and only the skim milk was used. Mother would put the skim milk in a large container on the back reservoir of the stove to warm until the milk clabbered. It was then poured into a tea towel and hung on the clothesline to allow the whey to drip out. After it had dripped dry, it was removed from the tea towel, moistened

with cream and salted and peppered to taste. Of course, the family mischief, Sam, was fond of tying bull snakes[1] together by their tails, throwing them over the clothesline and watching them fight. Whether going to hang clothes or cottage cheese out on the line, it was always frightening for mother to come upon these snakes.

There was one farm chore I was always unable to do in a competent or trustworthy manner. It generally was a chore delegated to the girls of the family and certainly one didn't need any coaching on how to gather the eggs in the henhouse. Just let one hen crane her neck at me or lightly peck me on the hand as I reached for her egg, and I would run screaming from their domain as if Indians had me in their eyesight and had already fired their arrows. Let a mother hen lower her head and start for me if she thought I was too near her baby chicks, and I would take off in the same manner.

The teasing and laughter I was subjected to because of this quirk was merciless and unbelievable in the family. Even the mean old white rooster knew of my plight and with the family looking on with great mirth, he sneaked up behind me one morning, and pounced upon my shoulders, digging in his spurs, and then flew onto the ground. That did it. Never again did I ever walk through that chicken yard without a club in my hand. It is still so to this day. All my life I have been completely "buffaloed" by a dumb chicken. The rooster wound up in a kettle one day, smothered in noodles. Mother had his three and a half inch spurs mounted and they look exactly like the horns on a Texas Longhorn steer. They are still in the family, but not mine.

This was also about the time the horseless carriage made its appearance on the homestead. Dad and mother bought a Model T. It was with great hilarity that we watched dad learn to drive. One day, dad came home and went to park the automobile in the shop. It was a great surprise to see the Model T go slowly into the front of the shop, quietly disappear and then come thundering through the back wall of the shop. As boards flew high into the air and the auto reappeared going at a full tilt, one could hear dad shouting "WHOA! WHOA!" Dad had confused the brake pedal with the gas pedal. For many days after that, the Model T would come to rest against a strategically-placed, heavy sandbag barricade.

Mother's driving experiences were short lived. One day when mother was touring along on the Indian Creek road, the wheel came off and went zipping along beside the car and off into the prairie. To my knowledge, mother never drove again.

---

[1] Non-poisonous species.

Bother Sam also had a chilling experience while driving a logging truck. On one trip down the steep mountain road with a full load of logs, the brakes on Sam's truck went out. Knowing he couldn't make it to the bottom of the mountain with the heavy load, Sam elected to jump from the speeding truck. The truck and its load went sailing over a ledge and were completely lost. When asked later why he didn't stick with the truck and try to save it, Sam's reply was an adamant, "They're still making trucks, but they're not making Sams anymore."

As automobiles became more and more common, the members of the family always competed with their vehicles. Each time a new auto was purchased, it was put the test – could it climb to the top of the steep hill east of the house? Time and again this feat was attempted, only to meet with dismal failure. It was finally brother Butch who purchased the automobile with the power to make it over the top.

XII   Harnessing the Wind

So it was that the depressing twenties and early thirties came and went. Many more changes were taking place in all areas of our lives as the thirties marched swiftly on. Only two or three of us were still attending school and continued to go to school until all the grades offered at the Beaver Creek School were completed. None of the children went on to a higher place of learning. We all learned the three R's and felt we had accomplished what was required at the time.

Of the remaining, unmarried eight children at the beginning of the decade, five including myself were married during the thirties, and moved on to nearby communities to make their fortune and raise their families. Incidentally, my mother and Leo Hillewaert, the young man with the accordion who had shared her first experience in the snowstorm going to the homestead in 1903, were to share in one of the weddings. Emma's son, John, married Leo's only daughter, Mary, in the 1930s.

It was during the early thirties that the wind was harnessed in the form of a wind charger. It was constructed in the backyard to charge the batteries that supplied the energy to wire the house with electric lights – six volt, no less – and also operated the radio in the corner of the living room. The outside world around us was now inside our home. Amos and Andy, Honey Boy and Sassafras, and Ma Perkins were quickly added to the family along with the world news.

Every Sunday, the married children and their families would come home to spend a few hours with mother and dad. If one of them didn't show up, mother would stew and fret and wonder if someone was ill at their house. This practice continued year after year, not only on Sundays but holidays as well. The bonds of family were and still remain very strong.

Late in 1939, war clouds began gathering once again in Europe. The radio was in constant use with news from abroad. Soon the Germans marched through Austria, Poland and on west to Belgium, Holland and France. England was fighting for her life. And then Japan pulled its sneak attack on Pearl Harbor, December 7, 1941. The whole Vyvey-Verplancke family was at one time or another that Sunday visiting at mother and dads. World War II was in progress and remained thusly four more long years. My youngest brother, Fox, enlisted in the Air Force at the age of 19 and spent those years as a propeller specialist in the United States Air Force.

His enlistment left mother, dad and one brother, Bert, at home to run the ever-growing ranch. Early in the forties, Bert married a local girl, Phyllis Everist, and they lived with mother and dad until their new log home was built very close to the old home. Bert has lived on the home place all of his life. Incidentally, René married Phyllis' sister, Betty Everist.

During the war, my husband and I moved from the Big Creek Ranch where we had made our home after marrying, to Rawlins where I have lived ever since. As my husband worked for the Union Pacific Railroad and was on the road with the mine-runs into Rock Springs for weeks at a time, I would drive to the ranch on Monday morning to help with the haying and return to Rawlins on Thursday or Friday of each week. More and more, harvesting equipment was becoming mechanized on the farms and ranches in the valley.

Grace on her comical old Model A.

I drove a comical old Model A Ford that had many quirks and ailments. It was my job to rake all the hay after it had been mowed by an elderly crippled gentleman who drove a team of horses and two-wheel mower. Bert and Dad took turns sweeping and stacking the hay to the old slide-stacker where I then had the job of driving the plunger team of horses to push the hay up the stacker and place it exactly where they want it on the haystack. Time passed quickly and the job was finished.

During this time, gasoline rationing was in effect and each week or so I would go to the War Ration Board and receive a quota of ration stamps so I would have gasoline to drive back and forth. During the haying season, the four of us would put up nine hundred tons of alfalfa and native hay. In the evening after haying all day, dad and Bert would continue with the final irrigating of the various grain crops.

I must tell you here of a strange truism about the various patches of grain, hay or potatoes on the ranch. From the beginning of the clearing of the sagebrush on the homestead, each piece of land was given a name as it was cleared. Always in acres, they were named the 11 acres, 5 acres, 17 acres, etc. In our "Do you remember?" sessions, the Vyvey-Verplancke family to this day refers to the various patches in this manner. We all know exactly where such and such an event took place.

Haying with a team of horses as described above.

I believe it was in January 1946 and the war was over that the youngest member of the family, Fox, was discharged from the Air Force and came home. A few years later, Fox married a local girl, Betty Herring, and they lived for a time with mother and dad. A smaller home was later built for mother and dad, next door to the original Vyvey homestead house. Fox and his family have lived all these years in the original home on the place.

With the completion of their new little home in 1947, mother and dad were to enjoy some modern conveniences. The R.E.A. power line was brought into the ranch and electricity was put into the new home. Also, indoor plumbing was added. After forty-four years, mother and dad had electricity and indoor plumbing. Shortly afterward, Fox and his family, and Bert and his family, made the same additions. Soon, the old outhouse, along with the Sears, Roebuck catalog, was retired.

XIII

The Blizzard of '49

Once again, in the early winter of 1949, total isolation was to grip the homestead and surrounding Beaver Creek area for several months. On the 29th of December 1948, the wind and snow joined forces, and the Blizzard of '49 began its long and monotonous sojourn in the valley. Day and night, the wind and snow howled, twisted and turned with the bitter cold of winter isolating the homestead from the outside world.

We had all, at one time or another, teased mother that her well-stocked pantry always reminded us of a country store. For two people, she always had an enormous amount of staples in her storeroom, we thought. It certainly came in good stead for the three families living so closely on the ranch during the blizzard. Luckily too, the large number of buildings and windbreaks were good for the protection of the cattle and small band of sheep being raised there. At some period everyday, the men struggled to free the snowbound animals.

Once or twice during short-lived letups in the fierce weather, Fox would ride a horse into Encampment for the newspapers, mail if it had been able to get to Encampment, and a few staples, if that, too, was available. As the hard, icy snow banks built up around the houses, only the roofs were visible from a short distance away.

Dad, Bert and Fox then took turns checking the houses at night in case a fire would break out from an overheated stove or mechanical problem with the heaters.

The deer in the nearby mountains were driven down to the flatlands and sought shelter and food on all the places in the Beaver Creek valley. The hills east of the Vyvey-Verplancke ranch and all through

the corrals and grounds were covered with deer. They would come up to the sidewalks between the homes and mother, from time to time, would feed them potato peelings from her doorway and was amazed they would eat them. We were all in the same boat. Evidently, the storm brought all living things together in a common bond, survival.

At one point in February, the Air Force was called into the county to make hay drops to feed the starving bands of sheep and cattle that were stranded. One morning, the drone of a large plane was heard overhead and all rushed out to see it go over. It was very low and the men were plainly visible inside the huge cargo plane as they pushed out bales of hay near the buildings. As the bales hit the icy snow banks, they exploded into the air and the wind blew the hay to Nebraska or elsewhere. No more drops were attempted in the valley.

In the middle of March of 1949, the weather began to subside and clearing skies began to make more and more of an appearance each day. The Blizzard of '49 had spent its fury. I was living in Rawlins during this time and every few days I would converse with mother by telephone as to conditions there and in Rawlins. The whole of the county was isolated by the grip of that blizzard. Never once were the country telephone lines out of order to the Beaver Creek Valley during this long siege.

The final phase of the great blizzard began at once when the United States Army moved into the county to open the roads to the ranches and towns in the county. This contingent arrived at the road into the Vyvey-Verplancke ranch off the highway to Walden, Colorado, on April 1, 1949. They were spotted coming with their huge bulldozers and tractors, clearing the one-mile road of the twenty to thirty foot snowdrifts blocking their path. Great activity took place inside the homes. The womenfolk prepared a huge meal for the welcome visitors making their way to the doors of the homestead. It took the Army six hours to open one mile of road. The hot food and short time of rest was greatly appreciated before moving on to resume their tasks at hand. They especially enjoyed the sight of hundreds of deer on the hillsides, watching their progress through the snowdrifts. The blizzard was over.

XIV
Trips to the Old Country

Early in 1950 Dad began plans to make a trip back to the Old Country, back to the little farm where he was born. He wanted very much to see his sisters, old friends and the country once again. His parents were gone, but many of his relatives besides his sisters still resided there and in northern France. Mother had no desire to return to Belgium; she wished to remain at home with her family. She had no family or friends left in Belgium, and a boat or an airplane for a means of transportation, were the means of the devil as far as she was concerned. It was fine if dad wanted to go, but she was not going and that was that.

The health examinations, smallpox shots and information needed for a passport was all a big nuisance to mother and seemed a bit ridiculous to her. After all, dad just wanted to go home for a visit, didn't he?

So, May 1, 1950 dad at the age of sixty-six and forty-three years after the day he had stepped from the stagecoach in Riverside, was taken to the airport in Denver to board a plane for the trip. After a stop in New York City to change to a Belgian airline, he was on Belgian soil in Brussels twenty-six hours later.

He made his way by train from Brussels to his sister's kitchen door in the seaport of Ostende on the North Sea. The visit to his homeland had begun and he actually wrote several letters to us in his own handwriting and in English, no less.

Three and a half weeks later, he returned home to America with all kinds of things to tell. He talked rapidly and with great joy, telling mom and the family of his trip. No one understood a word he was saying, as he was now speaking Flemish. We interrupted him time and again with the plea, "Please, tell us in English!" He would begin again in English, and just when it was really getting exciting, he would revert back to Flemish. Mother would finally shake her head in a negative gesture of disgust, turn her back and walk away, muttering, "He'll come around after a betcha," (betcha' being Walloon for a 'little while' in English). It was three or four days before he said everything in English again.

The trip had been a great joy for him and his narratives about the various members of his family, made us all realize we really did have aunts, uncles and cousins and deceased grandmothers and grandfathers in a far-off land. We really were like other people – our neighbors and our school friends. We had relatives other than the brothers and sisters of the immediate family. Our Aunt Julia Hayden had moved from the valley to Colorado and then to California when we children were very small. We were not to see her again until 1959, get to know her and visit with her.

In the late summer of 1956, the family was faced with another disaster. A major hailstorm descended upon the ranch, and in one swift, sweeping motion that lasted twenty-two minutes, all the fields were completely stripped of their crops. With heavy hearts, Charles, Emma and their friends, Kels and Ida Nichols, walked through completely destroyed fields. They talked of ways to recover the estimated $9000 loss and came up with the idea of buying turkeys to pick the smashed crops off the ground. They returned to the house and, true to form, Emma prepared a batch of her famous Belgian drop donuts[1] and served them to her guests and family. In the face of devastation, Emma's valiant pioneer spirit was emphasized in her words, "Don't worry, we'll get by." The turkeys were never purchased.

Several years later, dad wanted to return to his native Belgium, but this time he wanted me to accompany him. He wanted this very much and although mother still refused to return to Belgium herself, she wanted me to go with him in her place. They were both 74 years old at this time, and perhaps this played a part in their urging me to go with him. I said I would go and the wheels were once again set in motion. Passports, health examinations and smallpox vaccinations were begun and concluded.

Before our departure, mother felt it very important to have her

---

[1] EDITORS NOTE: Not much is known about the making of Belgian drop donuts except they were always mixed in a three pound coffee tin, contained raisins and after they were cooked, they were rolled in powdered sugar.

marriage blessed by the Catholic Church. So, on June 20, 1957, Father John Meyer of St. Joseph's Parish in Rawlins, Wyoming performed this blessing.

We departed from the Denver airport, May 20, 1958, and returned home July 2 of the same year. It was a trip I shall never forget.

The flight was only sixteen and a half hours on a turbo-prop plane. Jets were not in service until 1959. It was an eventful trip at all times, and although we were to fly non-stop from New York to Melsbrook airport in Belgium, the first events happened on the flight over the Atlantic. As we approached Shannon, Ireland, we encountered bad weather. In the buffeting we received, our plane developed some mechanical problems. We were informed by the captain that we were diverting from our course and would make an unscheduled landing in Manchester, England, some distance north of London for the plane's examination and repairs. We were told we would be met at the plane doors and escorted, en masse, to a private dining room and resting place. We would be served our breakfasts, and were not to leave this area at any time. We would then be escorted back to our plane in the same manner when all was ready and continue on our way to Belgium. All meals and responsibility were on Sylvania Airlines. It was a delightful experience. The cockney speaking waitresses and waiters were delightful, and the food was scrumptious and bountiful.

Once again, we boarded the plane and flew directly and very low over London. What a sight! After the White Cliffs of Dover, the English Channel and a small portion of northern France, there it was – Belgium. Lower and lower we flew. The Atomium, the structure that was the Belgium symbol of the 1958 World's Fair, loomed below in all its elegance at the edge of the Melsbrook Airport.

As we were taken to the Customs door, dad spotted our relatives overhead leaning over the railing, shouting their greetings of welcome. Our flight was four hours late, but they knew what had delayed our arrival. After we passed through the narrow hallway and our passport pictures were checked with our faces pressed against the peepholes to see if they matched, we were to be checked through customs.

As we passed slowly down the line and it came our turn, I discovered dad was not at my side. He had disappeared. I looked around to see where he was. He was nowhere in sight. The customs officer asked me a question, and I couldn't understand a word he was saying. The next few minutes were total frustration. I couldn't understand him, and he couldn't understand me. He tried everything and I tried everything including a few words I still remembered in Flemish. Nothing worked.

And then, a gentleman stepped to my side and asked me if he could assist with interpretation as he spoke English. I accepted his help gratefully and within minutes I was through customs. As we walked away, the man informed me that most of the inhabitants of Brussels spoke French and he could tell I was trying to communicate in Flemish.

This was quite a country, I thought, as I started out to find dad. Then, I heard his booming laughter and letting my ears be my guide, I walked up four or five steps and into the air terminal proper. There he was – smothered in bear hugs and kisses on both cheeks. He was being greeted by relatives. I stopped to watch this scene a few steps away and soon he saw me. As he reached for my hand, he told me why he had disappeared. He wanted me to experience firsthand the frustration of being faced with the same dilemma he had experienced so many years ago when he had arrived in America and couldn't understand the language either.

I will never forget the greeting at the airport, so warm and genuine and affectionate. It was truly a wonderful feeling to be greeted thusly by real, honest to goodness relatives of my very own. My uncle and two cousins spoke fluent English and so the language barrier was no problem from then on as many, many of the inhabitants of Belgium and France spoke it too. Dad was not exactly the best of interpreters for me as many times he would unthinkingly speak to me in Flemish or French and then in English. It didn't matter to them, but it was rather strange to ask them to interpret for my dad and me, don't you think?

Gathering up our bags, we made our way to my uncle's car and began our leisurely drive to the seacoast and Ostende. There was much gaiety, visiting and pointing out of interesting landmarks along the way. We traveled through Ghent and Bruges, and as we came near Bruges and our destination, excitement held me fast in its grip as full realization of where I was really came home to me.

My cousin, the driver of the car, seemed to suspect my eager anticipation and announced he was going to take a quick jaunt through one area of Bruges and continue on our way. It turned out to be quite a delayed jaunt and amused us all very much, except my cousin, the driver.

We were packed quite firmly into a 1956 Ford Sedan and were buzzing down a cobblestone street, dodging children playing in the street, fish peddlers with their dog-drawn carts, pedestrians, cyclists, a few tiny autos and then we met a horse-drawn wagon loaded with milk, bread and fresh fish. We came to a sudden effective halt. The driver of the horses began giving orders that the best exit from this situation was to the rear immediately – for us. There was no room for the horse-drawn wagon and our auto to pass. We backed the car more than a block with the horse and wagon nearly pushing us all the way. Reaching a place to turnoff, we headed for the highway and continued on our way.

We arrived at Aunt Ida's home about six in the evening, and as we entered, I was quite taken aback and surprised at the greeting there. The house was full of people, a huge table was set and wives were busy placing food on any bare spot they could find on the table. A very loud, strange-sounding voice kept repeating over and over, "I see you, I see you, I see you!" Looking around to see from whom it was coming, I spotted a huge parrot in a very large cage and realized it was him. My youngest cousin, John Billiaert, had taught him the three words in English, and at John's cue, the parrot performed for him. Mentally making a note in my mind that he was caged securely, I burst into laughter as did everyone else, I quickly felt at home and very welcome.

All at once, I had more aunts, uncles and cousins than I had ever known. Everyone there was a relative and some, who couldn't wait for us to visit them, had come from France to welcome us that first day in Europe. It was a gala evening and reminded me very much of home on Sunday and holidays. My first day in Belgium was a memorable experience, never to be forgotten. There were to be many memorable and delightful experiences for me. I shall tell you of a few, particularly those dealing with direct connection to my family and, of course, mother and dad and things they had told us when we were growing up.

A few days later, we decided to spend a long, cold rainy day at the World's Fair in Brussels. We left Ostende very early in the morning and arrived at the gates of the World's Fair a few hours later just as it was opening in the morning. We took a small shuttle bus from the gate directly to the pavilions and their displays from numerous nations of the world.

I particularly was very interested in visiting the section designated and displayed as Belgium, 1900. It was set aside a bit from the other countries, a huge pavilion near the Atomium. It was so very interesting to stand in the doorways of the small homes, shops, beer halls, and fish markets there and the marketplace in the middle of the small city it represented.

I watched the cobbler repairing shoes for his family as the children played on the floor at his feet. There were two cats in a rocking chair and his wife was preparing the noonday meal for her family. It was also most enjoyable to watch the coppersmith and silversmith pounding their metals into wares to be sold to those who wished to buy them. It was great fun to drop into the beer hall and have a small draft of Belgium beer or a glass of water, which was sold everywhere we went. Because of the below-sea level altitude of Belgium, water had to be bought. It was a real treat to stop in the little bakery and purchase a couple of Sucar D'Kringles that mother and dad had always talked about when we were kids. They are the small, fancy, crisp Belgium waffles laden with powdered sugar and thick, thick whipped cream. They are delicious. A Sucar D'Kringle equals our very common ice cream cone in popularity and are just as messy for the children to devour.

Late in the afternoon, after visiting nearly all the pavilions, a very unexpected, hilarious and embarrassing event took place. I shall tell you about it mainly as an insight into dad's gregarious, fun-loving personality and his ability to adjust to any situation immediately and enjoy it to the hilt.

We were just twenty to twenty-five feet from the entrance to the Canadian pavilion which was our destination at the moment. All at once, we were completely surrounded by a huge mass of people yelling, "Texas Cowboy! Texas Cowboy!" There stood dad in his three-piece suit, Gabardine topcoat, black walking dress shoes and a fancy black, carved and handmade leather cowboy hat made for him by Roy Welton of Saratoga. He had insisted on taking this unique hat with him on this trip. It was a beautiful piece of craftsmanship, but it was very much out of place as a possession of dad's. He never, never wore a cowboy hat to my knowledge. He always wore a small-brimmed stockman's Stetson as a dress hat or a battered and crumpled, sweat-stained felt hat.

There he stood, in a cowboy hat, laughingly and gaily letting men, women and children from all nations put the hat on in a rakish manner, and then pass it back to him.

The dismayed and embarrassed look on my face while trying to maintain my poise must have attributed to another twist in this event. As I glanced around for a quick escape route into the Canadian Pavilion, I stared straight into the faces of a contingent of Royal Canadian Mounties. They were standing straight and tall, side by side in front of their pavilion in their beautiful suits. All had little smiles playing on their faces. Their eyes assured me they too, were enjoying this little tableau very much.

As that precise moment, I felt a sharp tug on my coat sleeve.

Glancing quickly to see who it was, I was astounded to see a little man about thirty years old with a huge shopping bag in one hand and a little black beret on his head. In broken and faulty English, he asked for permission to make a picture of dad, now correctly referred to as "The Wyoming Cowboy." I gave the permission with a nod of my head

Charles, the Wyoming Cowboy.

and informed dad to keep the hat on his head and stand still. I was fascinated as the little man in the beret whipped out a pair of small scissors and two pieces of black paper. Snip! Snip! Snip! And he reached into the bag for two pieces of five inch by seven inch heavy white paper. Quickly and deftly, he pasted the snipped silhouette of the Wyoming Cowboy in the centers of these papers and handed them both to me with his thanks and compliments. As I stared at the pictures, I was astonished at the remarkable detail he had accomplished as to dad's age, his hat and his prominent features. At the bottom of the pictures was the man's name, SIZO, and the inscription, EXPO '58, Brussels, Belgium.

Dad was ready now to continue on our way. While we walked the next few feet to the doorway of the Canadian pavilion, I held one of the pictures up so that the Mounties could see it. As we passed, they smiled and the second to the last one winked and made a head motion to my rear. I glanced back over my shoulders and stopped dead in my tracks for a moment. SIZO was snipping at a furious clip. Outstretched hands were holding money up high as they were next in line for a silhouette of the Wyoming Cowboy in the leather cowboy hat. It was, to say the least, one way to make a quick buck, wouldn't you think?

As we drove back to Ostende late that night, the discussions of sights and sounds of that day always brought peals of laughter when we talked about the Wyoming Cowboy. Dad had a wonderful day and we all agreed so had we. Yes, I still have these two pictures and treasure them very highly.

Early one morning, Aunt Ida, Uncle Alfons, dad and I departed in the trusty Ford with no real destination in mind except I had expressed a desire to see the area of Belgium that my mother came from. We drove up the coast from Ostende, and our first stop was Zeebrugge. There was not much to see except water, a dock and a very desolate beach covered with sand dunes. We drove on to Knokke, where we talked to natives and took pictures of various landmarks as points of interest. We journeyed from there to Westkapelle and on to Moerkerke.

As we have no trace farther back than mother and her parents, we visited with many, many of the old timers inquiring about her family. As Uncle Alfons spoke several languages, he tried various avenues to learn something about anyone in her family. While he was very busy with this, I was prowling around talking pictures of numerous, old, old landmarks. As this area was heavily devastated in both world wars, and it is a small city compared to most in Belgium, there weren't too many landmarks. We learned nothing of the Vermeersch family and continued on our way to Moerkerke, several miles away. I took many pictures along the way, and when we arrived in Moerkerke, we followed the same procedure. Damage from the war was very evident here, and my picture taking proceeded in lively tourist fashion. The town hall, police headquarters, schools, churches, and storefronts, were in my lens from all angles. Nothing was learned here, and we continued on our way to Bruges, a short distance away.

Bruges is one of the major cities of Belgium. The marketplace, bridges, canals, old walls around the city, cathedral, town hall and

many, many places of interest were again the targets of my camera. The marketplace was a delight to me, and it was great fun purchasing laces, linens and what-have-you to take home with me. The highlight of the day's wonders was the two very aged ladies sitting on their straight-backed chairs making bobbin lace as the edging on handkerchiefs. There were so many tiny bobbins flying about in their fingers. The women were delightful and charming. With a great sprinkling of laughter, they conversed with dad, my aunt and uncle while their fingers fairly flew every moment.

We traveled the remaining twelve miles to Ostende, and it was well after dark when we arrived. We had only traveled fifty or sixty miles during the day, but it was one of the most enjoyable days in Belgium.

I would be remiss if I did not include two other expeditions in Europe which dealt entirely with the Vyvey family and were, to say the least, of great interest to me. Dad and I went to Eernegem, a distance of eight miles, with cousin Alfons as our driver in his small Fiat car. With a little oil poured over the three of us, we would have been sardines in a can. That Fiat was the smallest car I have ever been in, but it sure got around in great fashion.

Charles Vyvey's home in Belgium.

We drove directly to the farmhouse and small farm where dad was born and raised to adulthood. The living room wall at home had been graced with a picture of this house and grounds all our lives. I recognized it at once. As we drove up to the buildings and I made this announcement, dad was very pleased.

Very few buildings were there as land is very dear in Belgium and every inch was used to raise crops. The house and barn was one huge stone building with a slate roof. As we stopped at the front door, shutters were being closed over the windows and the top half of the front door also closed tightly over the closed bottom half.

Dad rapped on the door several times and spoke to the closed door assuring the lady inside we meant no harm. He explained who he was and what we were doing there. She was very determined, but so was he. My cousin and I got back in the car, quite sure we were not welcome, and I called for dad to follow. I don't think he even heard me. He tried a new tactic and asked where the man of the house was and could he please speak with him. The top half of the door cracked a little way, and they continued to converse quite rapidly for a moment. Suddenly, the lady of the house swung the upper half of the door wide open and, cupping her hands over her mouth, emitted a very loud and clear call to a field nearby. The lady and dad continued to converse, but it was in a different way, with laughter interspersed throughout. Within a few moments, an elderly gentleman and his daughter appeared from the fields. The lower half of the door was then swung wide and the three of them took us on a tour of the place. These people were not relatives.

Everything was neat and clean and utilized to the very limit. The buildings were centuries old. Since this visit, with the help of genealogy records, I have learned that five generations of Vyvey's were born and raised there and in each family, the first son was named Charles. In dad's family, they had a set of twins, a boy and a girl. The boy was named Charles and died at the age of two months. When dad was born, he was named Charles and was the only living son in the family. Dad's first son was named Charles and dad's youngest grandson was named Charles.

Four work horses, two cows and a calf, ten chickens and two hogs were the only animals on the place. Several huge walnut and pear trees were interspersed among the buildings and the small garden was loaded with vegetables, potatoes, strawberries, a few grape vines and several rows of corn. They showed us the huge block of cement where Big Bertha, the German gun, had been mounted.

After pictures were taken and a very warm 'thank you' was extended, we said our good-byes. The three of them lined up against the wall of the house and waved to us as far as we could see them. Dad's exhilaration and conversation on the way back to Ostende added a great feeling to my joy at having had the privilege of visiting this place. A very delightful day it was.

A few days later we left Belgium and went to Neufchatel, France, to visit with dad's sister and her family and many other nieces and nephews. We traveled extensively throughout northern France and south as far as Orleans. I shall tell you of one excursion that was very interesting. Dad's oldest sister, Leonie DeRynck, had lived in Neufchatel and later for many, many years in Illois, France. She was still alive when dad made his first trip in 1950 and he had visited with her at that time. She died in 1956 and was buried in Illois. Of course, we visited many of her family there and we also visited her and her husband's graves.

On this day, her son Charles took us to visit her home in the Normandy hills not far from LeHavre seaport and Dieppe, north of the Seine River. She had lived alone in the huge three story mansion for a number of years after her husband died and the children were all married.

Leonie was nearly sixty years old when the Germans took over France in World War II. Most of her children and their families lived in the same area. Shortly after the Germans occupied that area, they took over her mansion as German headquarters for their forces. In the hills surrounding the place, the Germans began the manufacture of the V-2 rockets and buzz bombs which were used in the awful siege on England. Fourteen years after the war ended, when I visited there, the high wire fences were still standing around the heavily wooded area where they launched these bombs and "Verboten" signs were every few feet on the fence.

When Leonie's home was taken over by the German command, she was given two rooms upstairs and allowed to live there alone until the war was nearly over and the Germans were routed from the area by the allied forces. She was totally isolated and saw none of her family during this time. The Germans treated her well as far as creature comforts were concerned. She had no radio and no means of communication with the outside world or with the Germans during this time. Some of the early, very erratic buzz bombs that were duds the Germans fired landed very near her home. She had no idea what they were.

One afternoon she watched from her window as the Germans hastily prepared to pull out. The next morning they were all gone, and she was completely alone. The house was not damaged or hit by the allied liberating forces or by the German occupation either.

Leonie lived out her life in this mansion, alone, tending her gardens, flowers and fruit trees to be close to her family. Charles DeRynck unlocked the front door and showed us the whole house which was left just as it was when she passed away. The Renaissance furniture was all in its place, fine china and crystal and silver and cooking utensils in the cupboards. It looked as if she still lived there but for the heavily shuttered windows and padlocked doors. As he lived nearby, Charles watched over the place. The day we were there, he picked a large basket of Royal Anne cherries from one of her fruit trees, and I took many pictures of the place and surrounding countryside.

We continued on our trip visiting Roan, Paris, and Orleans, and then dad began feeling poorly and wanted to go home. We returned to Ostende, Belgium, made arrangements to cut our sojourn short by a week and flew home in early July. This trip dad and I made is a memory I will always treasure very deeply. There was one remaining surprise and delight I was to experience connected with this trip.

Two weeks after we arrived home in the States, my husband, daughter and I went to mom and dad's to show the family the slide pictures of our trip. One of the pictures flashed on the screen and before I could say a word about it, mother jumped up and told us all about it. She was very excited and talked fast while she identified the church, churchyard, graveyard, monuments and the entrance to the church in Moerkerke, where she had worshipped and been married. She told us the entrance and the huge grave monuments so near its front door were the definite recognition she experienced as they flashed on the screen. I had several more shots of this church from different angles as I had deliberately done when I photographed each church in the area where she had lived in her young years.

It was a pleasant reward to see how happy these pictures made mother. I had brought her a glimpse of her childhood, and we talked of the area many times together afterward.

XV The Last Years

During the fifties and sixties, mother and dad enjoyed several trips together. She joined him in attending the stock show in Denver and visiting friends and a nephew, Bill Hayden, there. Dad had attended the stock show in Denver every year for nearly thirty-five years. They made several trips to Arizona, Nevada and to Los Angeles, California, from time to time, to visit Aunt Julia Hayden and see the sights.

They remained quite active during the summer months on the ranch; mother tending the many flowers and small garden she now had, dad helping the two sons, Bert and Fox, with the irrigating and tending of three or four fish ponds on the ranch.

Mother in her apron and the broom in her hand was a familiar sight as she would chase a chicken from her yard or a magpie that was too noisy. Dad, his pocket knife in his pocket and a shovel in his hand, was always somewhere near his fishponds. Every evening or so, the two of them would take the car and drive around the Beaver Creek loop looking at the crops, scenery and stock on their place and the neighbors' places. This is a very enjoyable drive, and all in the valley call it the Beaver Creek Loop.

For many years, mother had been called Mother Vyvey by many who knew her well. Now, they were called Grandma and Grandpa Vyvey by young and old alike in the valley.

In the middle of January, 1960, mother began ailing and stayed inside more and more under a doctor's care. In March, she left the ranch and was taken to Mercy Hospital in Denver where she continued to fail. She had never been hospitalized before in her lifetime but adjusted very well. Dad and I and Bert's wife, Phyllis, stayed with mother the three weeks she was there. At the end of March, she was brought back to Saratoga to daughter Lena's home as she could journey no farther and had to be near her doctor. Her only wish, as in the beginning at Riverside, so long ago, was to go home to the homestead.

At 7:00 p.m., April 20, 1960 at seventy-five years of age, mother passed away. All ten of her living children were at her bedside at Lena's that day. Mother lies at rest in the small country cemetery near Encampment.

A very dear and old friend wrote the following Eulogy and Obituary which appeared in the Saratoga Sun, the weekly newspaper of the valley.

MRS. CHARLES VYVEY, 75, DIED WEDNESDAY
By
Mrs. Carl Willford

"Once again the bell has tolled to summon a well-loved and respected member of Our Platte Valley family.

Mrs. Emma Vyvey, friend, neighbor, ranchwoman and for nearly 50 years has answered that call to the new life in the Great Beyond. Through the hourglass flow the sands of time, bearing away precious moments, treasured hours, and priceless years. With this ebbing tide dear friends *pass our way and are gone. Men follow their loved one as far as human feet may go, then they halt before that last closed door where fragrant memories arise and linger while the bygone years march by in swift review.*

The colorful life of Mrs. Vyvey leaves a rich store of memories for her family, her friends and neighbors and all who knew her.

She led a rugged life, characteristic of western ranch women. Her home had an open door to the traveler and a hand of welcome always extended to all who stood upon the threshold.

Mrs. Vyvey was a legend in the upper valley for her great heart, her energy, and hospitality. Surely this wonderful woman will be missed from her community for many a year.

Mrs. Emma Vyvey was born in Belgium, October 16, 1884, daughter of Mr. and Mrs. Joseph Vermeersch. She was first married to Peter Verplancke in Belgium in 1902. The couple soon came to Encampment to make their home.

Peter Verplancke died six years later and his widow married Charles Vyvey in 1911. The Vyveys owned and operated a ranch on Beaver Creek south of Encampment through all the consecutive years. There her children were born and raised and it was her abiding place until her last fatal illness. For the past few weeks she was cared for at her daughter's home in Saratoga, Mrs. Albert Armstrong. She passed away at 7:00 Wednesday evening, April 20.

Survivors to love and cherish the beloved mother and grandmother are her husband, Charles Vyvey, seven sons, Sam Verplancke of Saratoga, William Verplancke of Encampment, Carl, Albert and Arthur Vyvey, all of Encampment and John and René Vyvey of Saratoga; three daughters Mrs. Lena Armstrong of Saratoga, Mrs. Alice Evans of Encampment and Mrs. Grace Gregory of Rawlins.

In addition to her children this worthy woman proudly laid claim to 22 living grandchildren and 11 great grandchildren.

Mrs. Vyvey was a member of St. Ann's Catholic Church in Saratoga. It was her parting request that there would be no flowers in her memoriam but that those wishing to commemorate her would donate to the cancer fund – an expression typical of the great heart of this unselfish woman.

Funeral services are pending at the Conroy Funeral Home.

In closing, let us say that women like Mrs. Vyvey leave a lasting legacy to all who knew and shared her life. To live a good and useful life, loved and respected by all is a challenge to those who follow after, neighbors, friends, children. Like a well known character in an old poem, we think that her name will be entered in the Great good Book as "One who loved her fellow men." What better epitaph could there be?

After mother's death, time seemed to stand still as each of us adjusted in our private way to our great loss.

At the time of mother's death, the VX Ranch, as it was known, was being run as a three-way partnership between the two sons, Bert and Fox and mother and dad. The VX brand had been mother's brand for the stock from the time Peter Verplancke's demise and was first registered posthumously to Peter on December 29, 1909. Upon her death, the brand was passed on to Charles Vyvey.

Dad remained active in the operation of the ranch, helping with the irrigating, the calving and with lambing of the band of sheep that had been added to the livestock some years before. Horses were no longer being raised for work horses, only a few saddle horses remained for the work with the cattle. The mechanized machinery took over in the fields of hay and grain during the planting and harvesting of these crops.

During the ensuing years, dad traveled several times back to Belgium to visit his sisters there, and to Los Angeles to visit his sister, Julia Hayden. Every January he attended the Denver Stock Show, and his many friends there enjoyed much of the summer, camping and fishing at the reservoir and many ponds stocked with fish on the ranch.

The time came in the late sixties that he no longer had sisters living in Belgium and in 1969, the last one, Julia Hayden, passed away in Los Angeles with dad at her bedside.

In July of 1969, his nephew Alfons Billiaert and his wife, Teensy, made a trip from Belgium to the ranch for a visit with dad and his family. They were most impressed with three things about this country, Wyoming, that they talked of repeatedly: The blue, blue sky; the ability to see for miles and miles, and lightning in the sky that accompanies the threat of rain. They had never before seen lightning in the sky.

Shortly after his eighty-third birthday, dad liquidated his holdings and retired completely. He sold the ranch to the two sons, Bert and Fox, who had spent their entire lives on the place and retained only his small home. He continued to travel some, attend the Stock Show in Denver and visit with friends there every winter. His summers were spent at home, working with his shovel on the fish ponds, irrigating, and fishing with his friends.

On May 3, 1972, dad went to Saratoga for the ride with Phyllis, his daughter-in-law. He became ill while there and was admitted to Carbon County Memorial Hospital in Rawlins, later in the day. Like mother, he had never been hospitalized before in his lifetime.

His heavy brogue became very difficult for doctors and nurses to understand and vice-versa for him to understand them. I spent many days with him translating his needs and wants and calming him when necessary.

The day drew nearer and nearer when the move from the old Carbon County Hospital to the new Carbon County Hospital was to take place. The move was made on May 17, 1972. According to the rules and regulations of the move, the patients were to be moved in a few hours in the morning, and all visitors were banned from the premises until 10 o'clock. Dad was in critical conditions at this time and was moved in the ambulance with two doctors and a nurse in attendance. Dad passed away at 11:00 o'clock, May 17, 1972 at the age of eighty-eight. He was the first patent to expire in the new hospital in Rawlins.

Funeral services were held in St. Ann's Catholic Church, Saratoga, Wyoming, with the Reverend Eugene Sullivan as Celebrant. He is buried in the Encampment cemetery at the edge of town.

As the funeral procession neared the gate of the small country cemetery, a herd of twenty to twenty-five cattle blocked the entrance, and the procession was halted briefly until the gate was cleared of cattle. The family plot was at the north end of the cemetery. The cattle proceeded, just outside the fence, to the gravesite, stopped walking and lined up against the fence to watch what was taking place. At the moment Father Sullivan began the graveside ceremony, the cattle began lowing and mooing very fondly. They were only fifteen to twenty feet away from the gravesite and very few of Father Sullivan's words were heard above the lowing of the cattle. When the service was concluded, the cattle became quiet, turned from the fence and slowly ambled down the road.

Peter, Emma and Charles lie at rest, side by side, in this small country cemetery not over a mile and a half from where all three stepped from the stagecoach that brought them to the Encampment Valley so many years ago.

Epilogue

The VX Ranch, now owned by Vyvey Bros., Inc. is still operated as a working cattle ranch by Bert and Fox Vyvey. Fox lives in the original Vyvey homestead house as he has all sixty years of his life.

There are only two ranches in the Beaver Creek Valley left that are still owned and operated by members of the original homesteaders. One ranch is the Vyvey ranch and the other, the Platt ranch.

Since mother and dad's deaths, two of mother's daughters have also passed away. Helena died in November, 1972 and Alice died in November of 1974. There are eight members of the original Vyvey-Verplancke family still living to date, seven sons and one daughter.

Family gatherings, reunions and "bull-sessions" are still a part of the family and invariably held at the Old Homestead with lots of good food and picture taking. The eight survivors live within a radius of forty miles of each other and today, we range in age from sixty to seventy-five. The Vyvey-Verplancke family has grown to include 23 grandchildren, 40 great grandchildren and several great, great grandchildren.

Update Winter 2015:

Since the first publication of *Sagebrush, Gunnysacks and Bailing Wire* in 1982, the VX Ranch has left family ownership. Our family will always be grateful to Grace Vyvey Gregory and Sharyn Gregory Guthridge for writing this story and first publishing it.

Grandma's Cabin Books thanks Sharyn for allowing us to republish Aunt Grace's story. All proceeds will go to support the mission of Grandma's Cabin, serving the community and preserving history. Our work, not only to preserve the original homestead cabin, but also the history of our family continues.

Penny Vyvey Walters and Candy Vyvey Moulton

The original Verplancke homestead cabin.

The VX Ranch circa 1980. Bottom left hand corner – original Verplancke house; upper middle right hand house in trees – orginal Vyvey house.

ABOUT THE AUTHOR

Grace Carol Vyvey Gregory's early life is described in the book she wrote. Although Grace completed the eleven grades offered at the little Beaver Creek School, she never graduated from high school. She went to Rawlins to finish her twelfth grade, but in late March only two months from graduation, she went home – partly because she was homesick and partly because her mother needed her.

Grace was married on November 15, 1939 to Melvin Harold "Greg" Gregory, who was at that time a cowboy-mechanic on the Big Creek Ranch. They lived in the Valley only a short time before moving to Rawlins, Wyoming, where they lived the rest of their lives.

Greg was to become a sought-after mechanic and Grace was always a "crack" bookkeeper. A whiz with figures, she loved the challenge of setting up and keeping books.

On July 17, 1954, Grace was conditionally baptized a Catholic. She was a woman of unending talent, simplicity and perseverance. Throughout her life she never faultered in her devotion to the family of Vyvey-Verplancke. The book she wrote is her final tribute to this family and to generations to come.

Grace was preceded in death by her husband of 35 years on December 26, 1974. She finished writing this book on May 18, 1981 and on May 26, she was struck down by the cancer which claimed her life. She died on August 8, 1981 at the age of 61 in Cheyenne, Wyoming.

I feel her life can be summed up by her own last two words spoken only seconds before her death . . . "I love."

-Sharyn Gregory Guthridge

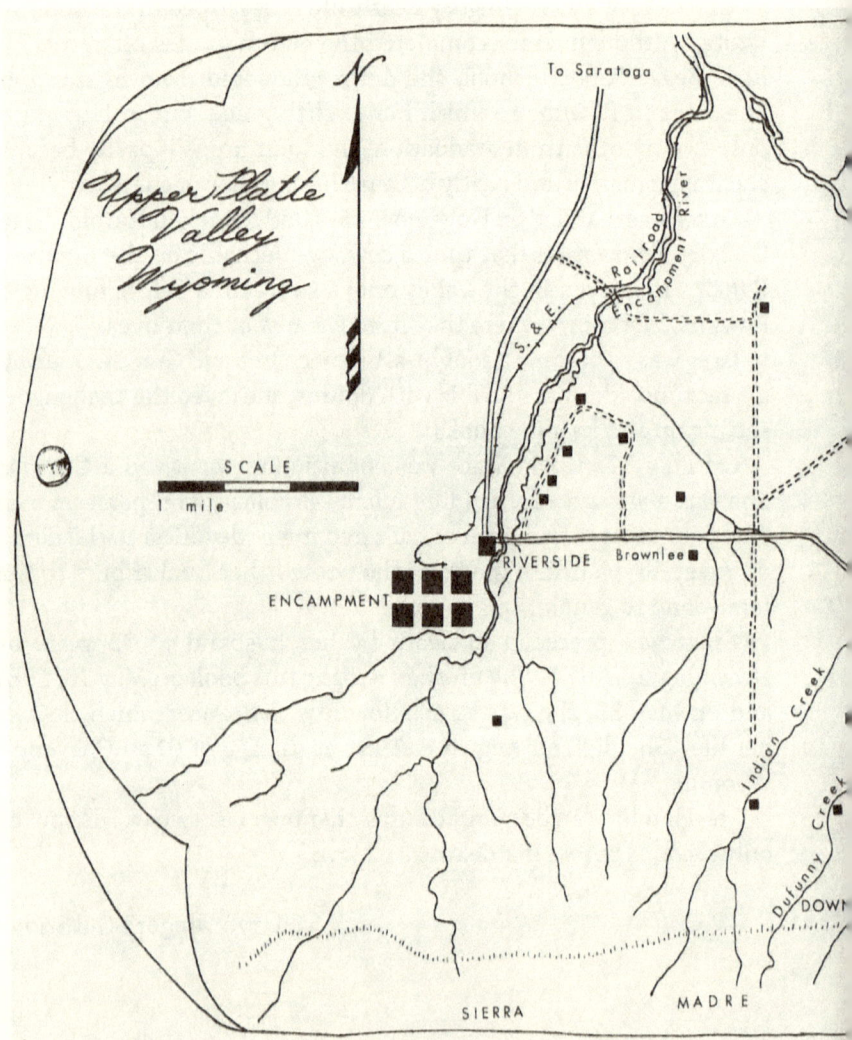

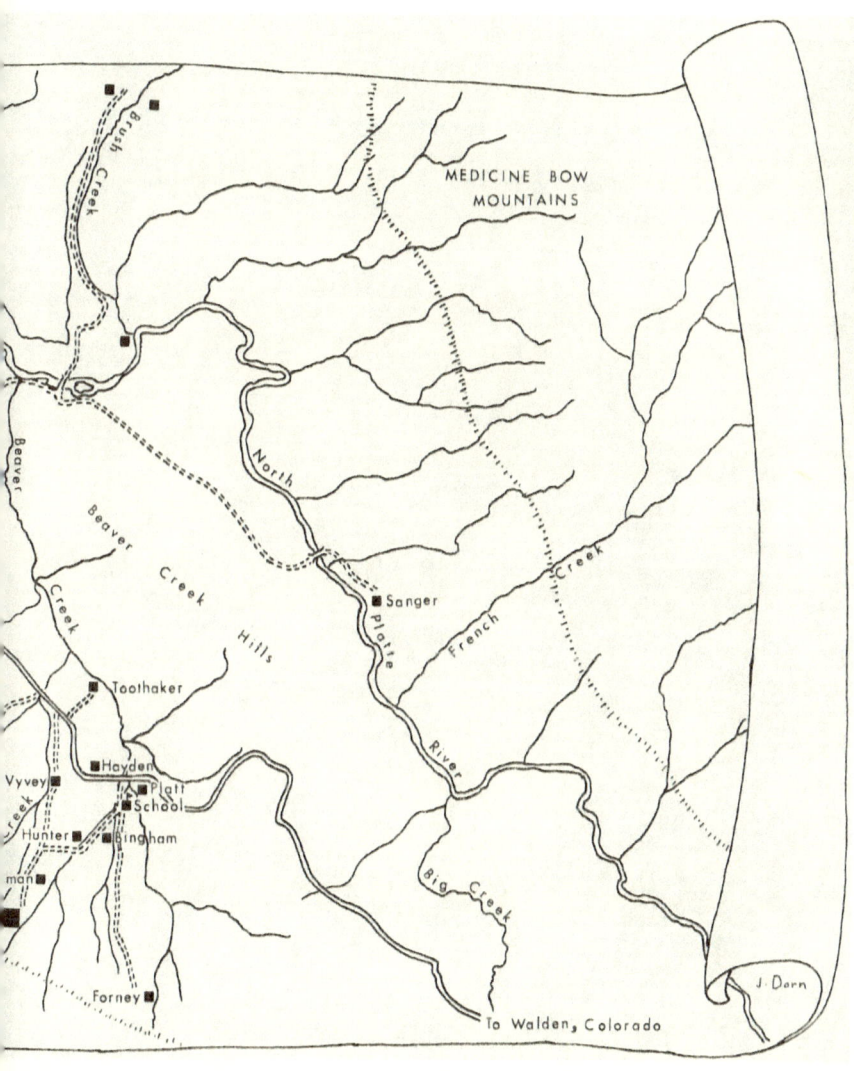

www.ingramcontent.com/pod-product-compliance
Lightning Source LLC
Chambersburg PA
CBHW030331080526
44584CB00012B/816